THE
CRUMBLING
WALL

What Is Wrong with Law Enforcement in America

KEVIN JOHNSON

Fulton Books, Inc.
Meadville, PA

Published by Fulton Books 2021

ISBN 978-1-64952-704-2 (paperback)
ISBN 978-1-64952-705-9 (digital)

Printed in the United States of America

CONTENTS

WELCOME, WHY, AND WRECKAGE

As I navigated my career as a law enforcement officer, I found it increasingly difficult to remain "one of the guys" while still serving and protecting the way I had always promised myself I would.

I had a choice to make, and I chose to serve and protect, and that made me less popular among my peers. I believe that I was respected for who I knew, for what I was able to accomplish at times, and for the relationship I had with the community.

But all too often, I was overlooked when it came to advancement, promotion, and the typical behaviors that were considered fun or dangerous that were relegated only to the boys club.

So why is that? We all get into this line of work to make a difference in someone's life, or so I thought. I know that I did. I found out over time that more than a few people get into this line of work because they are graduating college with debt beyond belief and no real job prospects. Colleges hold job fairs, and many police departments attend these job fairs with promises of tuition reimbursement, career advancement, and decent money for anyone who is young and in good shape.

So police departments are being flooded with recent college graduates, sometimes people dropping out of college for hopes of paying off some debt and getting into law enforcement as a stopgap measure to stem the tide of stresses from parents and professors.

Gone are the days of the police officer from birth whose only hope in life was to change the world. So we see the beginnings of the degradation of the heritage of the community police officer, the one who knows his whole life that he wants to serve his community and make his whole town proud.

Welcome the new and improved police officer who is college educated, full of vim and vigor, and anxious to prove to Mom and Dad that the immense amount of money spent on five years of college weren't wasted on drinking, hazing, and passable grades.

But there is one problem. The new officer doesn't go home to be a cop. He stays close to his friends or at least far enough from Mom and Dad to be his own man or woman. Why? Because we don't really want to go back to the town where the people knew us. That's why our new graduates don't live in the town he works in. Let's see what the excuses I have heard over the years are:

- "I don't want to work where I live. They will bother me while I am off."
- "I don't trust people to mess with my stuff when I am at work."
- "I don't want my kids going to public school where I work."

These are all signs that our new officers don't trust the public and don't command trust from the public.

So we have our first signs of disconnect from the community and the jurisdiction that we have sworn to protect and serve. Which, in essence, has eroded the actual statement that we are swearing to.

By definition, to swear is to bind oneself by oath.

By definition, an oath is to witness one's determination to speak the truth.

Now we have people who are working eight, ten, or twelve hours a day in a city they really have no emotional tie to, probably didn't attend high school in, and admittedly don't intend to send their children to school in serving and protecting our city.

Now, it's just a job. The best law enforcement officers never take this as a job but a career that they can't imagine not doing.

So to wrap up this section, let's talk about the wreckage. What has the disconnected officer created for those of us dedicated to the law enforcement lifestyle? How have they bastardized what we live or lived for?

I won't go into them in-depth, but I will give you a few examples.

1. A few officers were responding to a reckless-driving call when they used the app to determine if a woman would be arrested. Though the app landed on tails, indicating she'd be released, the officers decided to arrest her anyway. Roswell Police Chief Rusty Grant said he learned of the incident just before the July 4 holiday.
2. An ex-Hopewell cop got six years for sexual battery counts.
3. Three former Florida police officers were sentenced to prison this week for conspiring to falsely arrest people to improve the department's crime statistics at the instruction of their police chief.
4. Lieutenant Freddy Williams was charged with evidence tampering, possession of a controlled substance, and violating the rules of conduct by a county officer or employee—two felonies and a misdemeanor.
5. An East Greenbush police officer was arrested Tuesday and charged with possession of stolen property as part of an investigation by the state attorney general's office.
6. A Bonifay police officer was in custody after reportedly selling drugs out of his patrol car.
7. A police officer, who was one of them, was formerly employed with the City of Chesapeake for more than ten years. When the vehicle was searched, officials uncovered approximately three hundred pounds of high-grade marijuana with an approximate street value of $2,880,000.
8. A Bernice police officer had been arrested by the Union Parish sheriff's narcotics agents and charged with malfeasance in office and abuse of power.
9. The acting chief of the Sunray Police Department was being held on a charge of tampering with a governmental document.
10. A suspended East Greenwich police officer was accused of sending lewd text messages to a woman he had arrested earlier on the same day.

PROMISES TO THE PUBLIC

Richmond Police Department (Virginia)

Community-Focus

Accountability

Professionalism

Mission
We make Richmond a safer city through community policing and engagement.
Vision
The City of Richmond is a thriving community offering safe neighborhoods and an enhanced quality of life through responsive action, communication and public trust.

Shared Trust

Innovation

Integrity

Accountability
Community-Focus
Professionalism
Innovation
Integrity
Shared Trust

Mission

We make Richmond a safer city through community policing and engagement.

Vision

The City of Richmond is a thriving community offering safe neighborhoods and an enhanced quality of life through responsive action, communication, and public trust.

Atlanta Police Department

Mission Statement

The mission of the Atlanta Police Department is to create a safer Atlanta by reducing crime, ensuring the safety of our citizens and building trust in partnership with our community.

Vision Statement

We are a source of pride of the citizens of Atlanta, admired among law enforcement agencies worldwide, recognized for our professionalism, integrity and service to our communities.

Core Values

Professionalism: Taking pride in our actions, duties, development, and appearance

Integrity: Adhering to moral and ethical principles at all times

Commitment: Striving for excellence, accountability and effectiveness in our performance

Courage: Instilling trust and standing for justice in the face of danger

Raleigh Police Department (North Carolina)

Vision

The Raleigh Police Department promotes a positive level of real and perceived safety within the city of Raleigh that reflects a thriving atmosphere in which to live, work, and play.

Mission Statement

In the spirit of service, the Raleigh Police Department exists to preserve and improve the quality of life, instill peace, and protect property through unwavering attention to our duties in partnership with the community.

Columbia Police Department (South Carolina)
Mission and Vision

Our Mission

The Columbia Police Department will provide professional and ethical service in protection of our citizens while preventing crime and reducing the fear of crime through problem solving partnerships.

Our Vision

Through our steadfast commitment to policing excellence, the Columbia Police Department will be a professional, dynamic and innovative organization known for recruiting, hiring, training and developing an exceptional workforce that reflects the values and diversity of the City of Columbia.

Tallahassee Florida Police Department

The Tallahassee Police Department is driven by our core values—Trust, Loyalty, and Commitment.

Our values mandate that our decisions are based on what we should do, not what we can do.

Everyone at TPD is here to provide service to our community.

All members, sworn and civilian, have a responsibility to treat people with respect, show compassion, and protect the rights of all people.

We find a promise to serve the community and prevent crime and lots of other similar languages that make the public feel all warm and fuzzy, but in its core, we aren't even teaching our young officers how to do it.

We are making promises that we don't really intend to keep. If we intend to keep those promises, we will at least train to try to accomplish those missions.

In the Army, we used to say all the time, "You will act as you train, so train as you will act." We aren't teaching our young officers to successfully interact with the public, but we expect them to be able to do it.

And our administrators are never taught to do it, so they see no value in it. They have the I-never-did-it-so-why-should-they-need-it attitude. Or they have a warm-and-fuzzy attitude or a pat-the-public-on-their-asses-and-make-them-feel-better-about-society attitude that many young officers seem to have. Well, guess what, guys. We are public servants that may be called to calm the situation, and sometimes that means being warm and fuzzy.

That is why and how we are losing touch with our public. We only want to do the drive-fast-and-tackle-the-bad-guy stuff that makes us feel macho and like our heroes on TV.

WHAT CAN WE TRULY LEARN FROM TV COPS?

What did they do that was successful in thirty minutes minus commercials?

1. For nine years from 1960 to 1968, Andy Griffith mostly walked the streets of a small fictional North Carolina town without a gun but carrying something much more power-ful—the scowl of a true lawman and a real threat of action or redemption, your choice.
2. For seven seasons from 1982 to 1988, Cagney and Lacey were hard-charging feminist detectives working the streets and solving crimes, but they were relatable.
3. For six years from 1977 to 1983, we were blessed with *CHiPs*, showing the lives of two motor-cycle officers of the California Highway Patrol (CHP). Again, this was the sometimes fun and funny hijinks of two young officers living relatable lives on the screen for us to have a peek into.
4. For eight years, we had the *Barney Miller* show with its ten semi-main characters who gave us a glimpse into what a squad room might look like, and each of these ten charac-ters might be you or your family member. For twelve sea-

sons, the show and its cast were praised for its grittiness and realistic portrayal of their personal and professional lives.

Let's start with Andy Griffith. One of the greatest gifts that Andy and Barney brought to us in each and every episode was the difference between the letter of the law and the spirit of the law. We, as law enforcement officers, must realize that it is our job to do what is best for the community, and as law enforcement leadership, we have to allow our officers to know the difference and understand when it is important to acknowledge the difference without jumping down their throats for not writing that ticket or not arresting that person.

If you have ever watched *The Andy Griffith Show*, you know that the citizens of Mayberry had no respect for Barney Fife and his letter-of-the-law mentality. The only reason anyone listened to Barney at all was because of the respect they had for Andy.

Barney would often raise his voice in an attempt to try and gain respect, or in a few episodes, he would talk about getting new equipment because it would make it easier to control the influx of crime, just to have Andy confused over what crime he was talking about.

Cagney & Lacey showed us that female cops can be street-smart and intelligent. They have home lives and families and all the same problems that we have each and every day, and it broke down the mysterious walls of police work that many of us have possibly wondered about as children. They helped us to understand that police officers are people, too, and we can trust them, and we can actually like them too. Since police officers have all the same problems that we do, then they will have the same emotions that we do and experience all the same ups and downs and the same highs and lows on a semiregular basis that everyone does. Police officers can be vulnerable, whether they are men or women, and it is okay. Cagney and Lacey were tough as nails every day at work, and yet they were wives and mothers too. For many people, we had never seen that side of a police officer or detective before. So they helped us bridge a gap with society.

Well, what can I say about *CHiPs*. It was family friendly and fun. It had lots of car chases, crashes, and danger. You name it. But did you know that in six years of the cop show, there was only one police officer who ever drew his weapon? Patrol Officer Barry Baricza drew his weapon several times on the show. So in the dangerous climate of the California Highway Patrol, wouldn't you think that in six years, there would be a reason to draw your weapon once in a while?

Apparently, Ponch and Jon didn't think so. Season 1 alone had plot twists with everything from an auto theft ring to a biker gang, and yet no guns were drawn. No shoot-outs? Maybe, just maybe, the police can handle a desperate situation without violence? This is what we were raised on. This is what we know as normal. That is why it is so foreign to us when the police want to get violent and rude. It is not normal behavior to us.

The *Barney Miller* show brought us a detective bureau with the most racially mixed people ever seen on TV up until this point in history. It showed us how a racially diverse group of people should act toward each other and how the police act toward the public. We saw a bunch of police detectives who each in their own right probably would rather be doing something else. None of them really fought hard to solve crimes, but they did a good job. Not a great job, but a good job.

Barney was in charge of this multiracial group of detectives and had a knack for keeping everyone levelheaded and calm in the face of tragedy. The public loved him, but that caused him a lot of grief from his superiors, so he didn't get promoted as often as he should have.

So even back in the seventies, we had lessons to learn, both good and bad, from television law enforcement. The writing was on the wall of how community policing was being rejected by law enforcement administrations. Barney Miller was a successful cop in the eyes of the public, but to his police administrators, he garnered much ridicule for his public accomplishments. Why? We serve the public, so why are we held back for pleasing our bosses?

In May 1929, President Hoover appointed George W. Wickersham, the attorney general of the Taft administration, to head an eleven-member Law Observance and Enforcement Commission to study the implementation of the amendment and make recommendations.

A conflicted commission issued its findings, known as the *Wickersham Report*, in early 1931.

THE WICKERSHAM REPORT

The Report on Lawlessness in Law Enforcement

The only other Wickersham Commission report to gain any public attention upon release, and the only other one to be out of step with the orientation of the remaining reports, was the Report on Lawlessness in Law Enforcement.

In blunt and provocative language, the report declared that "*the third degree*—that is, the use of physical brutality, or other forms of cruelty, to obtain involuntary confessions or admissions—is widespread."

The abuses included "protracted questioning," "threats" and "intimidation," "physical brutality," "illegal detention," denial of access to counsel, and delay in producing a prisoner before a magistrate.

Local officials were unashamed about their methods. The Commissioner of Police in Buffalo said "if I have to violate the Constitution or my oath of office, I'll violate the Constitution."

Beatings of suspects were widespread across the country.

A suspect in Cleveland was forced to lie naked on the floor and then lifted several times by his sex organs.

The Detroit police used a practice called "around the loop," which involved moving arrestees from one of the fifteen precinct stations to another to keep him from family, friends, and legal representation.

The existence of the third degree was well known among local criminal justice officials, and at least some other members of the general public, but the Report on Lawlessness in Law Enforcement was the first time an authoritative government body had ever recognized and condemned it in print, with thorough documentation, gathered through field research and a national review of relevant court cases.

The report concluded with an evident attempt at balance by summarizing the "excuses" and "evils" of the third degree.

The excuses included that it "is necessary to get at the facts," and "is used only against the guilty"; that various "obstacles…make it almost impossible to obtain convictions" any other way; that it is "inevitable and…an excusable reaction to the brutality of criminals"; that restricting the third degree would "impair the morale of the police"; and that organized crime "renders traditional legal limitations outworn."

The evils, meanwhile, included that the third degree creates the "danger of false confession";

that it "impairs police efficiency" by discouraging professional police practices; that it impairs the efficiency of the courts; and finally that it "brutalizes the police, hardens the prisoner," and lowers public confidence in the criminal justice system.

The *report recommended some significant changes in criminal procedure*, some of which anticipated changes in the law by several decades, although it is not clear how they would address the third degree problem directly. The recommendations included establishing legal representation for defendants "in all cases" (which the Supreme Court would not require until the 1960s), requiring the prosecution to provide the defense with a list of its witnesses, eliminating race discrimination in jury lists (an issue that would wait until the civil rights movement of the 1960s), simplifying and clarifying the law on the admissibility of evidence, and others.

The recommendation to end race discrimination in jury lists, it might be noted, was one of only two occasions where a Wickersham Commission report addressed discrimination based on race, ethnicity, or national origins (the other being the Report on the Enforcement of the Deportation Laws of the United States, discussed below).

Earlier observations in the report, however, undercut the likely effectiveness of the recommended changes in criminal procedure with respect to the enormous problem of police lawlessness. Changing the law of criminal procedure, it had previously argued, would have only mini-

17

mal impact because officials either do not enforce existing law or deliberately disobey it. "Statutes cannot cope with the third degree nor can police regulations. Without the will to enforce them, these become words upon a printed page. The real remedy lies in the will of the community."

For this problem, however, the Wickersham Commission report had no recommendation. Other Wickersham Commission reports also noted the overriding importance of public attitudes, meaning specifically serious problems in the administration of justice. This was most evident in the Report on Prohibition, which noted the pervasive violation of the law and indifference to enforcement abuses.

The Report on Crime and the Foreign Born, meanwhile, noted the persistent public belief that immigrants committed crime at a disproportionate rate compared with native-born Americans, despite evidence to the contrary.

Citing public opinion as the fundamental problem was essentially a fatalistic conclusion, an admission that they had no immediate, practical reforms to recommend, and that they had no real answer to the question of how to change public attitudes.

The Report on Lawlessness in Law Enforcement stands out among the various Wickersham reports because of its explosive conclusions and its civil liberties orientation. No other report so bluntly accused public officials of pervasive wrongdoing. Other reports blamed problems on unqualified personnel, the influence of "politics," or sheer public indifference. There is, in fact, some mystery surrounding how the Report on Lawlessness in Law Enforcement was initiated and how its three co-authors were selected in the first place.

Co-author Walter Pollak was the ACLU's premier Supreme Court litigator in the 1920s and 1930s, arguing several landmark cases that marked the beginnings of the revolution in the law of individual rights. Most important, he argued Gitlow v. New York (1925), where the Court established the principle that the Fourteenth Amendment incorporated the First Amendment.

He also argued two Scottsboro cases, notably Powell v. Alabama (1932) where the Court held that Powell, facing a possible death penalty, had been denied due process of law because he had not had legal representation.

The Scottsboro affair, where nine young African-American men were accused of raping two white women near the small Alabama town of that name, and which involved numerous court proceedings over many years, became a national cause célèbre in the 1930s, and arguably the first great national civil rights case.

In addition to extending the principle of incorporation of the Bill of Rights into the Fourteenth Amendment, the Scottsboro cases marked the Court's growing attention to issues of racial justice. Coauthor Zechariah Chafee of Harvard Law School was the reigning authority on freedom of speech, based on his 1919 law review article and 1920 book on freedom of speech in wartime.

His views played a major role in shaping public opinion and the course of constitutional law in the direction of greater protection of freedom of speech in the years between the first and second world wars. He was also one of twelve prominent attorneys (including Felix Frankfurter and Roscoe Pound) who coauthored the report *Illegal Practices of the United States Department of Justice*, a stinging critique of the famous "Palmer Raids" of late 1919 and early 1920, where federal authorities arrested hundreds of alleged radicals.

Given the background and concerns of its authors, one could easily predict what kind of report they would write. No other Wickersham Commission report nor any of the crime commission reports of the 1920s involved the civil liberties perspective of the *Report on Lawlessness in Law Enforcement*. The surviving documents do not help to explain how these three individuals were selected for the report.

The most likely explanation for the origins of the *Report on Lawlessness in Law Enforcement* was the fact that Chafee was a Harvard Law School colleague of Roscoe Pound, the intellectual guiding force behind the Wickersham Commission, and also that Felix Frankfurter, a major figure in the crime commission movement and a founding member of the ACLU.

The nature of the lawlessness study did provoke some controversy within the Wickersham Commission, with some commissioners arguing over whether to continue it or publish a final report. Oddly, some evidence suggests that Commission Chairperson George W. Wickersham was not fully aware of what the report really involved.

Some commissioners adamantly objected to the entire enterprise and wanted the Commission not to publish any part of it.

Nonetheless, the report survived with its explosive evidence intact. The report arrived at a propitious moment in the history of police reform. In the 1930s, a new generation of reform police chiefs was coming to the fore and began taking the police professionalization movement to a new level.

The leader of this movement was O.W. Wilson. He began writing on the subject of police administration in the mid-1930s.

His book *Police Administration*, first published in 1950, eventually became the unofficial "bible" on the subject and shaped police thinking through the 1970s. To be sure, the *Wickersham Report on Lawlessness in Law Enforcement* hardly ended police misconduct. Police brutality erupted into a national controversy in the 1960s and misconduct continues today. But for the reform-minded police chiefs who emerged in the 1930s, the report served as a valuable point of reference and support. The *Report on Lawlessness in Law Enforcement* (the report discussing the use of the third degree) completely overshadowed the modest *Report on Police*, written by August Vollmer, then near the end of his career as the leader of the first era of the police professionalization movement.

It closely resembled other police investigations of the 1920s, including the relevant chapters of the various crime commissions, and reiterated what had developed as the standard prescription for police professionalization: the elimination of "politics," the hiring of experienced managers as police chiefs, and the improvement of police officer recruitment and training standards.

_____ This color indicates areas of surprise to me that were identified in this report.

_____ This color indicates areas of a call to action for the general public in this report.

_____ This color indicates areas of expected issues that were identified in this report.

So as I read over this Wickersham report, I find it alarmingly similar to issues that can be happening today. I think you can take this portion of the total report and put today's date on it and society will not totally think that it was from almost ninety years ago. Have we truly not progressed in law enforcement any further than that?

I am actually surprised to see some of the forward-thinking portions of this report that concerned the treatment of race relations and how they recommended that deportations be utilized back then, and yet it is still an issue today. So if we had actually taken the advice of President Herbert Hoover and this Wickersham Commission reports, perhaps we would have a better resolution to some of the issues we are having in the world today.

But why were there be some commissioners that adamantly objected to the publishing of this report?

It is my contention that "we the public" is the beginning, middle, and end of the problems in law enforcement, and this commission stated that. I think that was probably why the commissioners were afraid to publish this report. They stated in the report that the real remedy lies in the will of the community.

I have been telling the public for years that you will only be a victim of crimes when you sit back and allow yourselves to be victims. Criminals will take the path of least resistance, and if you stand up for yourself and make waves, they will find another path.

What is the difference? If your criminal is one in uniform, then stand up. Don't take it lying down. You have the advantage of technology today. Videotape your interaction with the police. I was videotaped on many occasions, and it never concerned me. I asked people to please step out of the area I was working to keep my personal safety, but I ignored the camera because it didn't change the job that I was doing. And guess what happened. Nothing. I still did the job that I was going to do anyway.

Police chiefs in most localities are hired and fired at the will of the jurisdiction's administration, and those administrations are elected officials.

Use your voice, speak up, and be heard. As I told people when I referred to crime, you can lie down and be a victim or you can stand up for yourself and stop it.

The Wickersham reports stand true to this day, and we should be thankful for our thirty-first president, but we should be ashamed of the commissioners who didn't want to publish this report and for the people who didn't or wouldn't take this advice.

When are we going to stop shooting ourselves in the foot and take our own advice? It is written in black and white and nearing one hundred years old, but we still insist on overseeing a society where we allow the very public officials, who are supposed to protect us, to physically and emotionally abuse us on a nearly daily basis. And what do we do? We shake our heads and condemn every hardworking, ground-pounding, blood-sweat-and-tears-giving man and woman who puts on the uniform. No. Praise the ones you know and love, but with that same energy and drive, condemn those that are bastardizing the life that I give my heart and soul for.

Don't just stand by and watch anyone get mistreated.

THE KERNER COMMISSION REPORT

President Lyndon Johnson formed an eleven-member National Advisory Commission on Civil Disorders in July 1967 to explain the riots that plagued cities each summer since 1964 and to provide recommendations for the future.

The commission's 1968 report, informally known as the *Kerner Report*, concluded that the nation was "moving toward two societies, one black, and one white—separate and unequal." Unless conditions were remedied, the commission warned, the country faced a "system of 'apartheid'" in its major cities.

President Johnson, however, rejected the recommendations.

The commission asked and answered three core questions.

What happened? Why did it happen? What can be done to prevent it from happening again?

So let's go to the beginning and discuss what the *Kerner Report* addressed and why the president of the United States felt it was so necessary to task this commission to look into the problems.

This commission was formed largely to address the racial issues across the United States in the 1960s. President Johnson wanted the three questions above answered, and the report answered those questions.

Rather than go over the entire report, you can read it here. I will go over the "Why did it happen" portion and perhaps relate it to what is happening today and see if there are lessons that we are once again not learning from our past.

Why Did It Happen?

The basic causes: The most fundamental is the racial attitude and behavior of White Americans toward Black Americans.

Race prejudice has shaped our history decisively; it now threatens to affect our future.

Frustrated hopes are the residue of the unfulfilled expectations aroused by the great judicial and legislative victories of the civil rights movement and the dramatic struggle for equal rights in the South.

This statement above is, to me, very poignant. For many people, even today, who are educated on the civil rights movement and who have been truly impacted by the education and teaching of people such as Dr. Martin Luther King Jr. and Malcolm X, I feel like they may find themselves having frustrated hopes as they are described by this report. So let's get back to the report, and remember that we are reading a report that is explaining a society that is already embroiled in racial divide. So we aren't necessarily dealing with a problem that is coming but what created this problem and where law enforcement went wrong.

The police are not merely a "spark" factor. To some African Americans, police have come to symbolize white power, white racism, and white repression. And the fact is that many police do reflect and express these white attitudes. The atmosphere of hostility and cynicism is reinforced by a widespread belief among African Americans in the existence of police brutality and in a "double standard" of justice and protection—one for African Americans and one for Whites.

What Can Be Done?

The community response

The commission recommends that local governments do the following:

- Develop Neighborhood Action Task Forces as joint community government efforts through which more effective communication can be achieved and improve the delivery of city services to low-income residents.

- Establish comprehensive grievance-response mechanisms in order to bring all public agencies under public scrutiny.
- Bring the institutions of local government closer to the people they serve by establishing neighborhood outlets for local, state, and federal administrative and public service agencies.
- Expand opportunities for low-income residents to participate in the formulation of public policy and the implementation of programs affecting them through improved political representation, creation of institutional channels for community action, expansion of legal services, and legislative hearings on neighborhood problems.

Police and the community

The abrasive relationship between the police and the minority communities has been a major and explosive source of grievance, tension, and disorder.

The blame must be shared by the total society.

The police are faced with demands for increased protection and service in all neighborhoods. Yet the aggressive patrol practices thought necessary to meet these demands themselves create tension and hostility. The resulting grievances have been further aggravated by the lack of effective mechanisms for handling complaints against the police.

Special programs for bettering police-community relations have been instituted, but these alone are not enough.

Police administrators, with the guidance of public officials and the support of the entire community, must take vigorous action to improve law enforcement and to decrease the potential for disorder.

The commission recommends that the city government and police authorities do the following:

- Review police operations in the low-income neighborhoods to ensure proper conduct by police officers and eliminate abrasive practices.

- Provide more adequate police protection to low-income residents to eliminate their high sense of insecurity and the belief of many African American citizens in the existence of a dual standard of law enforcement.

- Establish fair and effective mechanisms for the redress of grievances against the police and other municipal employees.

- Develop and adopt policy guidelines to assist officers in making critical decisions in areas where police conduct can create tension.

- Develop and use innovative programs to ensure widespread community support for law enforcement.

- Recruit more African Americans into the regular police force and review promotion policies to ensure fair promotion for African American officers.

- Establish a Community Service Officer program to attract low-income neighborhood youths between the ages of seventeen and twenty-one to police work. These junior officers would perform duties in their own neighborhoods but would not have full police authority.

The federal government should provide support equal to 90 percent of the costs of employing CSOs on the basis of one for every ten regular officers.

Control of disorder

Preserving civil peace is the first responsibility of government.

Unless the rule of law prevails, our society will lack not only order but also the environment essential to social and economic progress. The maintenance of civil order cannot be left to the police alone.

The police need guidance as well as support from mayors and other public officials. It is the responsibility of public officials to determine proper police policies, support adequate police standards for personnel and performance, and participate in planning for the control of disorders. To maintain control of incidents which could lead to disorders, the commission recommends that local officials do the following:

- Assign seasoned, well-trained policemen and supervisory officers to patrol low-income areas and to respond to disturbances.
- Develop plans which will quickly muster maximum police man power and highly qualified senior commanders at the outbreak of disorders.
- Provide special training in the prevention of disorders and prepare police for riot control and for operation in units, with adequate command and control and field communication for proper discipline and effectiveness.
- Develop guidelines governing the use of control equipment and provide alternatives to the use of lethal weapons. Federal support for research in this area is needed.
- Establish an intelligence system to provide police and other public officials with reliable information that may help to prevent the outbreak of a disorder and to institute effective control measures in the event a riot erupts.
- Develop continuing contacts with ghetto residents to make use of the forces for order which exist within the community.
- Establish machinery for neutralizing rumors and enabling African American leaders and residents to obtain the facts. Create special rumor details to collect, evaluate, and dispel rumors that may lead to a civil disorder.

The commission condemns moves to equip police departments with mass destruction weapons, such as automatic rifles, machine guns, and tanks. Weapons which are designed to destroy, not to control, have no place in densely populated urban communities.

So as I previously stated, President Lyndon B. Johnson rejected the recommendations of this report. But why? If you read this report in its entirety, you will see that it is full of life-changing ideas that could, and most likely would, have made a great impact on a large number of people.

I truly believe that although the ideas are even still a great idea to this day, at that time and even now, it is too much too fast. If the report had been filed with the president in perhaps layers or portions and recommended over a number of years, then perhaps it would have been better received.

But to bring the focus more on the law enforcement perspective in identifying what this report identified in 1968, over fifty years ago. The list of recommendations by this report are found above, and I cannot expand on them any better than how the author of the report stated it back then.

I found an extremely interesting article in the *Smithsonian* magazine dated March 1, 2018, "The 1968 Kerner Commission Got It Right, but Nobody Listened."

Released fifty years ago, the infamous report found that poverty and institutional racism were driving inner-city violence.

So if it was true back then and we understand that it is still true, then why don't we reread it and utilize the knowledge and understanding from our forefathers?

Kerner Commission Members

Otto Kerner, governor of Illinois and chair (D-IL)
John Lindsay, mayor of New York and vice chairman
(Republican who switched to Democrat in 1971)
Edward Brooke, senator (R-MA)
Fred R. Harris, senator (D-OK)
James Corman, congressman (D-CA)
William McCulloch, congressman (R-OH)
Charles Thornton, founder of defense contractor
Litton Industries
Roy Wilkins, executive director of the NAACP

I. W. Abel, president of US Steelworkers of America
Herbert Turner Jenkins, police chief, Atlanta,
Georgia
Katherine Graham Peden, commissioner of commerce, Kentucky
David Ginsburg, commission executive director
appointed by President Johnson

WHAT IS BULLYING AND WHO IS A BULLY?

Bullying is a distinctive pattern of harming and humiliating others, specifically those who are in some way smaller, weaker, and younger or in any way more vulnerable than the bully. Bullying is not garden-variety aggression; it is a deliberate and repeated attempt to cause harm to others of lesser power. It's a very durable behavioral style, largely because bullies get what they want—at least at first. Bullies are made, not born, and it happens at an early age, if the normal aggression of two-year-olds isn't handled with consistency.

Between one in four and one in three students in the United States reports being bullied at school, according to the National Center for Education Statistics and Bureau of Justice Statistics. In grades 6 through 12 alone, over a quarter of students have experienced bullying. Electronic bullying has become a significant problem in the past decade. The ubiquity of handheld and other devices affords bullies constant access to their prey, and harassment can often be carried out anonymously.

Just Who Is a Bully?

Studies show that bullies lack prosocial behavior, are untroubled by anxiety, and do not understand others' feelings. They misread the intentions of others, often imputing hostility in neutral situations. They typically see themselves quite positively. Those who chronically bully have strained relationships with parents and peers. Bullies can't exist without victims, and they don't pick on just anyone; those singled out lack assertiveness even in nonthreatening situations and

31

radiate fear long before they ever encounter a bully. Increasingly, children are growing up without the kinds of play experiences in which children develop social skills and learn how to solve social problems.

Police Training in Interviewing
and Interrogation Methods: A
Comparison of Techniques Used with
Adult and Juvenile Suspects
Juvenile Interrogation Training and Practice

The concern often raised by scholars and youth advocates is that interrogators are using the same psychologically coercive interrogation techniques with juveniles as they use with adult suspects.

Their primary findings were that psychologically coercive, Reid like techniques were used frequently and that rates of technique usage did not differ for child versus youth versus adult suspects.

Law enforcement interrogation trainings are not adequately preparing officers for the unique challenges of interviewing youth. ("Law and Human Behavior," *American Psychological Association* 40, no. 3 (2016), 270–284, http://dx.doi.org/10.1037/lhb0000175.)

Finding the Truth: Interview and
Interrogation Training Simulations
Interservice/Industry Training, Simulation,
and Education Conference (I/ITSEC) 2011

Proxemics is the reactions of an individual or groups of individuals with relation to the immediate surrounding area including the animate or inanimate objects within that area. Edward Hall described four aspects of space in his seminal work, The Hidden Dimension, including: Intimate space, personal space, social distance and public distance (Hall, 1966). An individual's personal space ("comfort zone") varies but in the U.S., it may range around 2 feet (varies in an individual side, front and back).

 OR

 OR

 OR

These images represent three things: bullying, gang intimidation, and police interview and interrogation.

I find them incredibly similar.

So why does bullying and school violence go on and we appear to have no idea how to address it? Maybe because we don't know how to tell someone not to do what we do.

If it walks like a duck and quacks like a duck, then it's—

Bullying and interrogation techniques are incredibly similar. I was just going over some of the more well-known and sought-after classes for interview and interrogation, and they all seem to push several of the same steps in the interrogation process.

1. Imply guilt
2. Keep them in an uncomfortable place
3. Give them a chance to explain but not deny
4. Interrupt if they deny

It is incredibly sad, but these are the first few basic steps to police interrogation techniques, and in most cases, they work just fine. So in the mind of a police officer, why wouldn't you go with what works? Well, you don't go with this when dealing with all people because you are not interrogating all people.

There are seven types of bullying.

1. Individual
2. Physical
3. Verbal
4. Relational
5. Cyber
6. Collective
7. Mobbing

How can each of these techniques be translated into the behaviors we have seen out of police officers every day?

1. Individual—made-up traffic infraction
2. Physical—aggressive arrest techniques
3. Verbal—cursing at suspects
4. Relational—spousal abuse
5. Cyber—threatening messages or texts
6. Collective—another coworker watches someone or somewhere
7. Mobbing—having several coworkers bully someone

Now that you see it in these terms, does it seem so farfetched to think that the police and law enforcement are built on a climate of bullying?

The heat lamps, the smoky rooms, the refusal to provide any food or drink for hours at a time? Of course, that is not true; that is just what you see on TV when they do an interrogation. But with interrogation comes isolation, fear, sometimes anger, desperation, and many more emotions that trained law enforcement officers know how to play off, and they utilize those skills to sometimes bully someone into a false confession.

Police Bullying Examples

Individual—made-up traffic infraction

> Police officer fired after unwarranted traffic stop involving daughter's boyfriend.

> Ohio police officer John Kovach violated the department's standards of conduct during the incident, his department said.

NEWS

This was published on June 22, 2018.

Physical—aggressive arrest techniques

DeLand Officer Fired for
Rough, Improper Arrest
Patricio G. Balona
December 3, 2018, 1:02 p.m.

After a law firm hired by [citizen] Kidd notified the department over the summer that they were planning to sue, officials at the DeLand Police Department viewed body cam videos and discovered that a trainee officer's accounts of what happened at the scene and what Officer Mulero [arresting officer] wrote in his charging affidavit were inaccurate, investigators said.

Verbal—cursing at suspects

Video Shows Orlando Police Officer
Threatening, Cursing at Man in Truck
Officer Under Internal Affairs Investigation
Erik von Ancken, Anchor/Reporter
February 20, 2017, 4:09 p.m.

An Orlando police officer has been reassigned after a video of him cursing and yelling at a man in a threatening manner went viral on social media.

Relational—spousal abuse

Police Chief Knew of Spousal Abuse
Austin Fisher, *Sun* Staff Writer, August 16, 2018

Carlos violated a Santa Fe Police Department directive when he chose not to report allegations that a sergeant under his command choked and punched a girlfriend in the back of the head, Santa Fe police records show.

When asked if Carlos informed her that he was going to report it to his superiors or to the Santa Fe police chief, she said Carlos told her, "He, he wasn't gonna report it to anybody."

Cyber—threatening messages or texts

Former Philly Cop Gets Prison Time for Hundreds of Threatening Text Messages
Michael Tanenbaum, *PhillyVoice* staff, September 10, 2018

Another text was sent to E.W. two days later:

Is [E.W.'s daughter] worth the p***y it would be a shame for her to be fatherless I know everything about your dumb ass.

Collective—another coworker watches someone or somewhere

Asian Woman Records Police Officer
'Bullying' Her Black Boyfriend
Carl Samson, May 17, 2018

"I followed you because I remembered you. You're a dangerous guy," the officer said with a smirk.

The man can be seen calling his lawyer twice in the video, with the first call ending up in voice mail.

As he did this, the officer can be heard telling a colleague, "Oh, he's trying to get me fired."

The man succeeds calling his lawyer the second time, at which point the officers started heading back to their car.

NEXTSHARK

Mobbing—having several coworkers bully someone

6 Green Bay Officers Disciplined
for Harassment, Bullying
February 28, 2018, 12:26 p.m., *Associated Press*

As many as nine officers harassed and bullied eight colleagues on the night shift in 2016, including using racial slurs and other inappropriate conduct while on duty.

So Who Gets Bullied in Police Work?

Who Gets Targeted?

Like their child/adolescent counterparts, adult bullies are opportunistic and always like to have a target for their aggression. Driven by personal or professional insecurities, weak ego strength, and a desire to assert authority or bolster their own status, adult bullies prey on those they perceive as threats.

Studies demonstrate the victims of adult bullies tend to have certain shared characteristics, including: excelling at their job, often exceeding their bullies in competence; are popular, well-liked, and often at the center of attention; possessing high morals and integrity, as well as a strong work ethic; and, perhaps most telling, are not likely to fight back against the behavior.

Workplace bullies compensate for their own real or feared weaknesses by trying to eliminate or marginalize those they sense are better, might make them look "bad", or receive more attention.

Bullying in any environment is toxic, but in a police environment it may be especially toxic, and is a source of much of the low morale described by officers of all ranks. (Althea Olson and Mike Wasilewski, "Bullies in the Workplace: Sabotaging Police Culture," *More Than a Cop*, January 28, 2015.)

CHIEFS' SPEECHES

Full Text of Police Chief's Acceptance Speech
Casey McNerthney, June 24, 2010

Police Chief John Diaz and Seattle Mayor Mike McGinn at a
Thursday news briefing. (Casey McNerthney/seattlepi.com)

John Diaz, who has served as Seattle's interim police chief since
March 2009, is in line to become Seattle's new police chief.

Mayor Mike McGinn picked Diaz instead of East Palo Alto,
Calif., Police Chief Ron Davis.

"We have real leadership here," McGinn said at a Thursday
morning news briefing. The Seattle City Council must confirm the
pick.

Here is the full text of Diaz's remarks:

> I would like to thank Mayor McGinn for the opportunity to continue to lead one of the finest police departments in the country.
>
> It is no secret that I feel that policing is one of noblest professions that a person can undertake. It has incredible rewards and responsibilities.
>
> I have to thank the great chiefs that I've worked for through my 30 years, from Pat Fitzsimons to Gil Kerlikowske. My nomination sends a powerful message to the newest rookie on up to our most experienced professionals that you can aspire to lead this organization.
>
> I started as a patrol officer, I always think of myself as a patrol officer, and now every Seattle Police Officer can see a path in their professional lives that could lead to the Chief's office.
>
> This last year has been one of great challenges. We had an eight-day span that started with a neighborhood was paralyzed by fear of a serial arsonist and ending with the calculated execution of Officer Tim Brenton. These horrible crimes were solved quickly with the great work of the officers and the close cooperation of our community. During all of this time we did not have time to grieve. Officers continued to handle 911 calls which continued into December with Officer Ben Kelly stopping a fugitive who had executed the four officers in Lakewood. In the midst of all of this we successfully went through our third national accredita-

tion audit by the Commission on Accreditation for Law Enforcement Agencies (CALEA).

It is of no surprise to anyone who reads the paper and sees the news that our department has been tested and criticized in recent months. I want you all to know that in a progressive department we take this scrutiny seriously and take the responsibility to address our challenges and shortcomings. The plain truth of it is that no one is harder on the Seattle Police Department than itself. And the other truth is that we can only succeed in keeping our community safe by working with, for and through the community.

To this end, we are in the midst of an ambitious initiative to survey every neighborhood in the city to determine the crime and disorder priorities from a community perspective. We call this the "Neighborhood Viewpoint", and it is central to the SPD neighborhood policing plan. This expresses our philosophy that every neighborhood has different needs and priorities and that police services need to be delivered in a way that is responsive to our community.

The controversial incidents and the recent upsurge in violence during the late night and early morning weekend hours has my full attention and commitment to address these issues and reaffirm the high standards for which this department is nationally known.

And finally this is our opportunity to rededicate our focus on our highest mission—unfailing public safety service to the citizens of Seattle.

I cannot end this without thanking my wife Linda, a 23 year veteran of the department for her support. When I put on this uniform every day I can't help but think of the work the men and women of this department do and I can't thank them enough.

Thank you again Mayor McGinn, I will go back to my desk this morning as we have deployment issues, budget and other matters to continue to deal with.

New Oakland Police Chief Sworn In, Promising to Make City Safe
Kimberly Veklerov
Updated 6:08 p.m. PST, Monday, February 27, 2017

Anne Kirkpatrick was sworn in as Oakland police chief Monday, casting herself as a truth teller to push the city department toward progress after years of periodic turbulence and a procession of leaders who tried, and sometimes failed, to implement reforms in the troubled force.

Kirkpatrick, 57, is the first woman to hold the top position in the Oakland Police Department. In a short speech delivered inside the council chambers of City Hall, she promised to reduce crime—her "true north" goal—and mend fractured relationships with the community.

"We know where the goal line is," she said during the ceremony. "We know how to get there. So now all we have to do is go."

Kirkpatrick was an outsider pick—a status made unmistakable by her distinct Southern twang.

"You are a charmer, and now we can add Memphis to the list of languages that are spoken in Oakland," Mayor Libby Schaaf said during the ceremony, referring to Kirkpatrick's hometown and the city in which she first put on a police badge.

Toward the beginning of her career, Kirkpatrick moved to Washington state, earning a law degree from Seattle University and climbing the ranks to be police chief of three departments and second-in-command of the King County Sheriff's Office. Last year, she went to Chicago to lead the Police Department's Bureau of Professional Standards as the city worked on reforms after the shooting of Laquan McDonald, a black teen killed by a white officer.

Kirkpatrick began interviewing for the Oakland job soon after she got to the Windy City and before the bulk of the outlined reforms could be realized. Schaaf said Monday that during an interview, she was impressed with Kirkpatrick's take on the "broken windows" philosophy of policing— she said that law enforcement should address quality-of-life issues without overreaching into disadvantaged communities—and with her response to how she wanted to be known as a chief.

"You said you hoped to be remembered as a decent woman with good values—a pioneer who restored the nobility of policing," Schaaf said.

In Oakland, Kirkpatrick finds a department beset with challenges and one still licking its wounds from a series of recent scandals, the biggest of which involved allegations that several officers had sexual relations with a sexually exploited teen. That episode, amid swirling questions of who knew what and when, led to the departure of Kirkpatrick's predecessor, Sean Whent. Two successors each lasted only days.

Schaaf, calling the department a "frat house" with a "toxic, macho culture," in June appointed a civilian, City Administrator Sabrina Landreth, to run the agency while a nationwide search was conducted for a permanent chief.

The handling of the misconduct case drew a sharp rebuke from the federal judge who has overseen the department for the last 14 years, after the city settled a landmark civil rights case involving the corruption and abuses of four officers in West Oakland. The scandal threatened to prolong the court oversight, which appeared to be coming to an end, and caused morale within the ranks to plunge.

While Kirkpatrick joins a department still under court oversight, in some ways it's a new era for the city and its relationship to the police. In November, voters overwhelmingly approved a citizen-led police commission with the authority to fire the chief.

Kirkpatrick, who told The Chronicle she looked forward to working with the commission, didn't touch on the past controversies at City Hall, telling reporters, "History is a part of our fabric, but we've got to look to the future."

The heads of the Piedmont, Berkeley, Emeryville and San Leandro police departments as well as the Alameda County Sheriff's Office attended the ceremony, as did Alameda County District Attorney Nancy O'Malley.

Noticeably absent were some members of the Oakland City Council and Fire Chief Teresa Deloach Reed, who had gone on leave last month, came back to the office briefly, but was on leave again Monday, sources said.

In an interview with The Chronicle last week, Kirkpatrick said that creating bonds between the police and community must center on day-to-day interactions.

"When you walk into the police department, how you get treated at the counter makes a big difference," she said, citing her frustrating experience getting a California driver's license at a Department of Motor Vehicles' branch last week.

While the Oakland force has a challenged relationship with the community, she said, it's "hard to be a police officer in America right now."

"It doesn't matter if it's Oakland or Chicago or a town you've never heard of," she said in the interview. "Being a police officer in America today is tough."

Kirkpatrick told reporters that she wasn't "a quitter" and has long been drawn to the Oakland agency—a sense illustrated by the fact that it wasn't her first time applying for the job.

Councilman Abel Guillén said her persistence was possibly the most promising part about her appointment. Kirkpatrick's choice to live in Oakland, unlike some predecessors who lived outside city limits, was assuring, too, he said.

"The fact that she re-applied says a lot to me," he said. "She wants to be in this city... Her ability to walk to work and see neighbors just like other Oaklanders says a lot for me, and that's a welcome change from the perspective of the community."

William Bratton's First Speech
Chief to Enforce Vision
Bratton Shares Mayor's Reformed Goals for Department

Here is Los Angeles Police Department Chief-designate William Bratton's full statement Thursday:

I did not bring my interpreter with me, so I hope the Boston accent with some New York nuances will not be too difficult to understand. But I'm certainly going to work on changing that so that I can fit more closely into this city.

I want to thank the mayor from the bottom of my heart, both personally and professionally, for the opportunity that he is presenting to work

with him to implement a vision that he has artic-
ulated so well for what this city can be, what it is
capable of achieving.

And I cannot even begin to express to you the
pride I feel at having been chosen from among
this stellar group of police professionals that
applied for this position. Some of the best and
brightest in American policing sought to lead
what is widely perceived to be one of the best and
brightest police departments in this profession.

John Timoney, Art Lopez. To be in the company
of such individuals is an honor in and of itself.
But to be selected from that group for this assignment is something that I am eternally grateful for.

The mayor has talked about his vision. The
reason I applied for this position—to return to
public service, an area that I love and which I
enjoyed so much when I was in public service
for so many years—is because that vision is a
shared one. The belief that community policing
is the philosophy that needs to be embraced by
America's police forces and one that the LAPD
has expressed so much support for—its unions,
its leadership, its rank and file, and, certainly, the
citizens of L.A.—have responded to the vision of
community policing that I share with the mayor.
Partnership, problem-solving, prevention, with
the emphasis on prevention.

The LAPD, in the '60s and '70s, the era when
I was first coming into the business—32 years
ago, October 7th, 1970, I joined the Boston Police
Department as a 23-year-old recruit, one day

after my 23rd birthday. I had grown up on images of the LAPD, 'Dragnet,' 'Badge 714,' 'Adam 12.' All of the TV shows of that era celebrated an organization that set the standard, for so many years, of the profession that I wanted to join.

And the professional model of policing that shaped so much of the '70s and '80s was designed and implemented here. That model, which emphasized rapid response, random patrol and reactive investigation, for 30 years was the model. But now community policing has shown itself to be much more effective in reducing crime and disorder and fear.

And the goals of the LAPD, the goals of this mayor, are quite clearly by embracing community policing, by building on the foundation of the consent decree. He has referenced that it is a foundation and not the ceiling, and it will be more than a foundation. It will be integral to everything that we do in the LAPD during my time as police chief, as I believe deeply that the department and the city, officers and citizens, will benefit from the consent decree and its quick and full implementation.

I had the privilege of spending almost a year working as one of the monitors, an opportunity to get into the LAPD in a very intimate way, and that intimacy is what propelled me to apply for this position. The intimacy with just how good this department is, how truly extraordinary the men and women of this organization are.

It had its couple of tough years, but I think it's fitting that this ceremony is being held here in this station, in the division where the LAPD, in one of its finest hours, exhibited what it is truly capable of and what it is desirous of doing. Putting itself between the danger and the citizens. The thin blue line. That term was created here by a former chief, and it's appropriate because it's a city that has very few police. But with very few police, it makes up for that with the professionalism and the skill of its members.

Chief Pomeroy, who was rightfully applauded by all of you, is a perfect example of that. I feel honored to be able to succeed him and all he has done over these intervening months to hold this department together in very critical times. Marty, I know how much you love this place, and I promise you and the other 9,000 LAPD and all that came before you that I will not let you down, this mayor will not let you down, that together we will build on the legacy and the traditions and the skills. And we will take that—the most famous shield, the most famous badge in the world—and whatever little varnish, a little tarnish exists, it will be wiped clean, and that it will be the most brilliantly shining badge of any in the United States.

That's our commitment to you and to the members of the LAPD. And to citizens, the mayor has made it quite clear—that he will not tolerate abuse, racial profiling, anything that does not, in fact, work to prevent crime and disorder and the safety of all citizens of all colors and ethnicities.

Mr. Mayor, I cannot extend to you or to the members of the Police Commission enough thanks for the honor that you are bestowing on me. And my compliments to the members of the Police Commission on the process that you put us through. I've gone through a lot of processes, and I've never gone through one that was as comprehensive and, I might point out, as fair as what you put together and which we responded to. It was reflective of this city and this department and the commission—a truly professional endeavor, one that I think I benefited from because I had to prepare for it. And in that preparation, I think I am much better prepared for the position that you are allowing me to go before the City Council to seek to attain.

New Morrisville Police Chief Sworn In as Officers, Family Fill Town Hall

Morrisville

As town clerk Erin Hudson guided Patrice Andrews through the ceremonial oath of office Thursday, the new police chief had to compose herself before repeating the first few lines.

Andrews, in her speech following the oath, thanked her colleagues and family, including her grandmother, who passed away two years ago from the day of the ceremony, for everything they had done to help her become police chief. But she also clearly felt the gravity of her personal accomplishments—those of a relatively young officer who became the first black woman chosen to lead the fast-growing town's police department.

"As I stand here today, I can't believe I was the same girl from Chapel Hill many years ago, the same girl who, at 22, took a risk and responded to an ad in the paper—when you could actually open the paper and read it—seeking Durham police applicants," said Andrews, 42. "But I realize I'm not that same girl. I stand before you a woman that's had many experiences, learned many lessons and risen through the ranks to be where I am today, and I deserve every bit of it."

The former captain with Durham's police department was announced in April as Morrisville's next chief of police. Andrews began work June 6 and took her official oath in private June 7. "This is more just for pomp and circumstance," Andrews said of Thursday's ceremony, which began with a bagpipe-and-drum performance by the Morrisville Honor Guard.

She took over from interim Police Chief Felicia Sykes, a captain with the Morrisville Police Department who assumed the chief's duties when Ira Jones retired last year after being chief for 11 years. Sykes was awarded the department's Officer of the Year award earlier this month for her work as interim chief.

Andrews' family and friends alone took up about a quarter of the available seats in the Morrisville

Town Hall chambers, where the ceremony took place. She was joined on stage by her husband, Chris Andrews, a corporal with the Durham Police Department.

The crowd appeared to approach or exceed the capacity prescribed by the chamber's fire code, in part because of the dozens of area fire and police officers who had come to Town Hall to see Andrews sworn in.

"The strength of your service is shown by the number of officers who attended today," Councilman Satish Garimella said. "That really speaks well of you."

Mayor Mark Stohlman addressed some of those officers in his remarks, especially Andrews' former colleagues from the Durham Police Department.

"I had the honor of talking today with your former boss, Durham Mayor Bill Bell," Stohlman said. "We always have friendly rivalries, and I told him, 'I think I got you on this one.'"

Andrews has highlighted community and data-driven policing as her primary focuses as she begins work in Morrisville. She's also taking over a police department that's set to add new officers this upcoming fiscal year for the first time since 2008, thanks in part to lobbying efforts by Town Manager Martha Paige during this most recent budget cycle.

"Any time a community is growing as quickly as Morrisville is, your police department needs to be keeping up with that growth," Andrews said. "You definitely don't want to over police, but...adding more resources gives officers more opportunity to grow. You can reorganize your departments, you can add ranks. I do share those concerns, but the fact that the town manager recognizes that, as well as the council, goes a long way to helping me transition and plan for the future."

Andrews and her family will move into a rental property in Cary before purchasing a home in Morrisville next year, a decision Andrews said she wanted to delay until she's settled into her new job.

Official remarks ended with the belated arrival of Councilman Michael Schlink, whose words of welcome were particularly apt given what will perhaps be Andrews' greatest challenge:

"Sorry," he said. "Got caught in traffic."

Somerset Holds Swearing-In Ceremony for New Police Chief Tuesday Night
McNeil Formally Accepts 3-Year Contract with Starting Salary of $115,000

Somerset—George McNeil, a 28-year police officer in Randolph, became the town's police chief after being sworn in with a signed contract during a brief ceremony Tuesday night in the Somerset Middle School auditorium.

Looking both relieved and excited, McNeil received an enthusiastic ovation as his mother, Toni McNeil, who is improving in a battle against leukemia, pinned the chief's badge to her son's lapel.

Brockton District Court Judge Kathryn White, a colleague of McNeil's, administered McNeil's oath while he placed his hand on a Bible held by Tarnya, his wife.

"I cannot express to you enough the pride and honor I feel being the chief of this wonderful town. I am dedicated in continuing to make Somerset a great place to live and raise a family," McNeil said in a 3-minute speech.

He recognized on stage with him three police chiefs, including Randolph Chief William Pace; two other Randolph officers and two Somerset Police Department captains, Glenn Neto and Stephen Moniz. Moniz had also sought the chief's job.

"I think he's a very good communicator, good administratively and someone who can talk with the average person and connect with them," Pace said after the swearing-in. Pace joined Randolph's force with McNeil and vied for the chief's job with him a few years ago.

With a vast majority of the Somerset Police Department and its reserve officers in an audience of nearly 100, McNeil praised his new fellow officers for making Somerset "one of the safest communities in southeastern Massachusetts."

He vowed to continue the community policing and partnerships that have been a bedrock of the town force.

With a new Board of Selectmen that has changed members in each of the past three years, and whose unanimous vote for McNeil as an out-of-town candidate to make changes elicited some protests, the new chief briefly addressed those issues.

"As we develop programs, implement technology and take on new initiatives, know that the Somerset Police Department regards the town's residents as its highest priority," he said.

He said they'd "continue to build on our traditions of honor, professionalism, integrity and dedication."

"I want this police department to be as transparent as possible and never be involved in politics," McNeil said at the end of his speech. A standing ovation followed.

That concluded a 15-minute ceremony, which began with Board of Selectmen Chairman Donald Setters and Selectmen David Berube and Scott Lebeau formally approving and signing the three-year contract of six pages that they verbally reached last week.

The salary is $115,000, with raises in 2016 and 2017 in accord with the department.

Each selectman offered comments after signing.

"We have full confidence you will be a great leader of this department and you will move it forward. Congratulations," Setters said.

Berube praised McNeil's energy and enthusiasm, and said he admired "people who are willing to make changes and changes for the better."

"That's why I voted for you," Berube said.

Lebeau, who chaired the search committee that began organizing in March after Joseph Ferreira announced his retirement after nine years as chief, called McNeil's appointment "the end of a thorough and successful journey."

Identifying the tradition of distinguished police chiefs, Lebeau said, "George McNeil is the perfect choice to continue and enhance the standard of excellence we have come to expect from our police department."

Neto, who graduated from the police academy with McNeil nearly three decades ago, said he knew the new chief as "a hard worker and very dedicated."

"In our brief time together (recently), I don't think that's changed at all," Neto said.

Asked about an out-of-town chief taking the helm, Neto said, "I think the caliber of the men and women of the Somerset Police Department are going to make it an easy transition for him to come in and work. They've all told me in conversations they're here to support the new chief."

McNeil, 50, of Bridgewater, also was joined by his oldest child, Nichole McNeil, 22, and three stepchildren, Jack, 11, Caroline, 13, and Christopher

Moitoza, 19. His son, Kenneth McNeil, 21, is serving in an Army training unit overseas.

"He's worked so hard his entire career," Tarnya McNeil said. "I know he's going to be the leader of this town that they're looking for. We're excited to become part of the community."

A meet-and-greet for the new chief, with light refreshments, followed the ceremony.

 Swears in New Police Chief

Torrington—the three stars pinned to the uniform of Torrington's new police Chief William Baldwin Monday have a special meaning, he said: They represent his sons.

In a moving speech to a standing-room only crowd at the Torrington City Auditorium, Baldwin thanked his wife, Susan; his three young-adult sons, David, Michael and Nicholas; and his father, William Baldwin Sr.

In his remarks to colleagues and the public, Baldwin said, "Every community gets the law enforcement it insists on." Baldwin pledged to support his native city. "I believe Torrington holds the distinction as the finest police department in the state," he said.

He started his law enforcement career with the Torrington Police Department in 1983, Baldwin said. He then worked for the Connecticut State Police until returning home to the city's department nearly 29 years later.

"It's unique to leave a place where you started and come back, especially as a police chief," he said.

Litchfield County State's Attorney David Shepack has known Baldwin for decades. He drew a laugh when he continued "and decades...and decades."

"Bill is a straightforward, ethical, honest and a skilled law enforcement officer," Shepack said.

"He grasps that law enforcement has changed over the years, as has the perception and obligations... Chief Bill Baldwin has a nice ring to it," he said.

"I'm pleased to administer the oath of office today," said Mayor Elinor Carbone. "The chief has an internal drive to support the community."

She complimented Baldwin for his "good strong sense of ethics and respect for the law."

Carbone also recognized Interim Police Chief Wayne Newkirk. "We were in fine hands with his role in the most difficult time. Wayne has done a fine job and earned respect."

Newkirk was named interim chief after former Chief Michael Maniago retired in June. He was chief for nine years.

When the announcement was made about Baldwin's hiring in November, Carbone said he was one of three finalists out of a group of 10 applicants interviewed for the position.

When the hiring process concluded, Newkirk was asked whether he was interested in the position.

"I have 24 years on the job," Newkirk said. "I plan on retiring soon. It's best if they bring in somebody."

"My career has been rewarding, both personally and professionally," Baldwin said "I have seen tragedy and been at (crime) scenes that made national news."

"I began my career here and I will likely end my career here as a police officer," he said.

It's Official: Fort Myers Has a New Police Chief

City council approved Derrick Diggs to take over the role after an intensive, year-long search. He spoke out about what he will bring to the job.

A year-long process was chiseled down to a two-second vote inside chamber halls.

City manager Saeed Kazemi said in his search for a new chief he wanted a new perspective, and they got it from a Fort Myers outsider.

Honor, ethics, accountability, respect, team-work—you can't miss the words written across the top of the Fort Myers Police Department.

New police Chief Derrick Diggs says he will bring heart to his new role at FMPD.

"We got several issues to work on. I'm going to be a very busy person, and we'll get through it," Diggs said.

As Diggs entered council chambers for the last time as a civilian, he shook hands with nearly every person inside the room.

He said it's this type of involvement that will turn around the perception of the department—where too often officers say witnesses won't help solve crimes.

Following the search that widdled down from eight candidates, Diggs now brings more than 30 years of experience as a police officer. He was also the police chief in Toledo, Ohio for three years.

Diggs retired two years ago, and wants back in on the job in Southwest Florida.

"This is what I do. I'm a cop. I'm a chief," Diggs said.

Neighbors said he has a lot to accomplish in a city where unsolved murders have spiked in recent years.

"That's the biggest thing…the unsolved murders have to get solved. So hopefully, he can clean up the streets and get murderers off the streets," one resident said.

"Being who he is and his background, he'll make a change for the better," another resident said.

Diggs said he's a technology-oriented officer. He said the public can expect to see that once he's officially on the job.

"I believe in using technology, both qualitative and quantitative data in addressing crime in the community," Diggs said.

Interim police Chief Dennis Eads got a standing ovation for his work in the last year.

Common Themes Discussed During New Police Chief Welcome Speeches

- "Close cooperation of our community"
- "By working with, for and through the community"
- "Survey every neighborhood in the city"
- "From a community perspective"
- "Delivered in a way that is responsive to our community"
- "Mend fractured relationships with the community"
- "From the perspective of the community"
- "Community policing has shown itself to be much more effective"
- "Clearly by embracing community policing"

So if this is the idea going into a job, what happens once they get there? I can tell you. It's the two sides of the coin effect. Heads I win, tails you lose. The community wants to know the police and wants the police to succeed. They want to be able to reach out and touch the police and know that they can trust the police. So the new chiefs and leaders assigned to the communities  make these grandiose speeches about how they are going to work better with the community and "clearly by embracing community policing," but when it is time to "put the rubber to the road," as they say, the Police (1) don't know how to do it and (2) don't like to do it.

But why, you might ask? Because community policing is up front, and in-your-face, results-driven policing requires officers to do a few things:

- Be accountable for themselves
- Be accountable for their time
- Be results oriented

- Be a source for information and understanding
- Have answers
- Be personable and relatable

Officers are great at what they do, but they are rarely good at being held to a timeline. We hated being given deadlines and just wanted to respond to a crime, catch the bad guy, and close the case. We liked what we saw on TV: drive fast, run after the bad guy, tackle him, wrestle around on the ground, maybe throw some punches, get dirty, put them in handcuffs, and take the bad guy to jail. Filling out paperwork was like the unfortunate part that came with all the fun stuff, and we usually got paid overtime for going to court, so that was extra money.

But community policing isn't any of the things I listed above. I have described community policing as the easiest job in police work and the one that police officers claim not to know how to do. You go to your assigned area and just talk to people. Ask them what you want the police to do, and assuming they are not telling you to get lost, you do what they need you to do. That is community policing. If you go to people and they don't want you to do anything, you have still done your job. Just keep asking people what they need done, and keep doing it.

You keep track of what you have done, what you have been asked to do, and what has happened to the crime rate in your area.

A perfect example was when I had the great luck of working for an interim chief of police, James Stanley, one time who had a program that he liked to call the CAP program, Community Action Policing. I was assigned to the Heights of Hopewell, and he said to me, "Fix what is wrong with the Heights. You know what to do."

I was told to work forty hours a week. I could make my own schedule, change my days off, come in riding a bicycle, or wear plain clothes, whatever. Just provide him with feedback on what I was doing and fix the Heights.

This, of course, pissed off some of the lieutenants and sergeants because they felt like I had too much control, and they wanted to be able to tell me what to work and when to work, so after the chief took care of that, I was off to do my job. I spent much of the first couple of weeks surveying the neighborhood and talking to people. The patrol sergeants and officers asked me a lot of questions, like "What are you doing?"

My response was simple, "Finding out what I am supposed to do. I can't fix a problem if I don't know what the problem is." So I worked all three shifts, talked to as many people as possible, and got as much feedback as possible to see what the problems were. Then I spent a few days at the headquarters on the computer, pulling crime stats and gathering information on what had occurred over the last twelve months, to see what the police department and the City of Hopewell thought the problems were.

So I was off to a good start gathering information and getting ready to start fixing the Heights, and I would report to the chief what I was doing, and he was fine with it, but some of the administrative staff were more than a little confused as to why I was on this special assignment to fix the Heights, and I had not even gotten out there and started making arrests yet. This showed a total lack of understanding of community policing.

So now I went back out into the community and spent about another week doing a review of the makeup of the community. How many single-family homes were there? Apartments? Duplexes? Empty lots? Abandoned properties? Businesses? Then I went to the real estate assessor's office and found out who owned all the possibly troublesome properties. I met with code enforcement to see if they were working on any of the properties in the Heights, and if not, I informed them of the troublesome properties and asked them to open up a work report to get started. I sent letters to all the businesses, churches, and landlords to inform them that I was assigned to their neighborhood and that I was excited to be in a position to help make any requests that they might have in the neighborhood a reality.

So now, I was about five to six weeks into my assignment, and I hadn't really started any enforcement actions yet. But the public had seen a lot of me, the property owners had seen a lot of me, the churches had seen a lot of me, and the bad guys had seen a lot of me. I had come in wearing plain clothes, rode in unmarked cars, rode on bicycles, and walked the beat, you name it. I had been a regular fixture in the Heights, and I am starting to see something.

People were used to seeing me, they knew my name, they knew my car number, and they welcomed my presence in the neighborhood. Kids came and greeted me as I walked around the neighborhood. I carried stickers in my pocket sometimes, so the kids always asked. I knew when the school busses ran, so I was out and in the area sometimes when the kids got off the bus. Even the drug dealers appreciated that.

So I reviewed all the information that I had collected over the first four to six weeks I was working, and something really interesting was discovered. The crime stats from the last twelve months, the things that I thought were the problems, and the citizen surveys all showed very different things.

We have to remember that in order to do a good job to the public, we have to address the problems that they think are the problems. If I stop all jaywalking in your neighborhood and you don't give a crap about jaywalking, how satisfied are you going to be with my service to the community? When I got started with this CAP program, I would have thought that the primary concern would be drug dealing, vandalism to vehicles, and larcenies. The crime stats showed that the biggest problems in the area were burglaries, drugs, and larcenies. But the citizen surveys showed that by far, the biggest complaint in the neighborhood was that citizens hated when people left their trash cans at the street after the trash came.

Yes, you read that right. They wanted the trash cans brought up from the street after the trash ran. So I called the trash company and checked with the city code, and technically, they had twenty-four hours to remove the can from the street. The trash company agreed to put stickers on the cans to let people know what the law was. I put flyers on the cans that were left on the street, and I identified who was elderly and physically disabled, and between myself and the neighborhood watch, we would go and take up the trash cans for the people who could not physically do it for themselves. Eventually, the trash men ended up doing it for us for the few that couldn't do it for themselves.

Within two weeks of getting the stickers on the cans, the citizens were calling the mayor and praising the police department for the great work that we were doing in the Heights. Not me, per se, but the police department. A lot of people thought it was stupid, but many more thought it was great, and that was who we are there to service, the many more. So I continued to expand on the survey, and after around four months, I repeated the survey and reviewed the information and did the same thing.

See in community policing, you are establishing or reestablishing pride in the community that gives people a voice. Crime only lives where there are no voices. Crime takes the path of least resistance, and if you stand up for your community, criminals will find a less-resistant community. We must instill a sense of pride in our community if we want to make people proud of where they live.

CPTED (Crime Prevention through Environmental Design) is one of the most important methods any police department can use to control crime and one that is least used anywhere. I will give a few examples of what I have done.

I was assigned to public housing and was working the Piper Square Public Housing Area. I had been walking around the area, as I did every day that I worked, and noted that at in one specific apartment, the residents always came in and out the back door. I spoke to the woman and asked why she came out the back, and she said that she was afraid of the people always hanging out by her end of the building where it was dark, and the grass got high, so she never knew if there were snakes in there. I asked her if she minded if I trimmed up the shrubs in front of her windows. She advised me that they were there when she moved in, and she didn't care about them.

The next day, I came to work in some scrubby clothes, and I dug up all the shrubs, trimmed the hell out of the short tree that was in front of her apartment, and cleared the entire walkway leading up to her apartment. People came out of all the apartments around to ask what the heck I was doing. I told them that I was helping out the community by making the area cleaner and getting rid of some problems because I had seen some snakes and rats in the area. The reason for this was to keep from making it look like the resident was working with the police and to guarantee that the drug dealers didn't come back. No drug dealer is going to hang where someone has seen rats and snakes. They just didn't realize that the rats and snakes I was talking about were the drug dealers.

Another instance of me using CPTED was when Davisville Housing Community had a problem with trash always being on the ground. Well, I would be out in the area, and every now and then, I would catch someone throwing trash on the ground, and I would make them pick it up or threaten to write them a summons for littering, but that really created no long-term solution at all. So I started thinking. There needed to be trash cans all over Davisville that the Housing Authority could come around maybe daily and empty, or they could have community service through the courts and have people empty the cans. So I went over to see where to put the cans, and when I got there, I was stunned. There were already trash cans there, and I had totally missed them. There were four trash cans already in place that were empty. So I took a picture of them. They were so windblown and old that they just naturally disappeared into the background of the area. They were the metal-type outdoor cans that were attached to a pole that was cemented in the ground.

So I went to the local department store (Roses), and for ninety-nine cents each, I purchased five cans of fire-engine red spray paint. I took the trash cans off the poles, painted them fire-engine red, and put them back on the pole. I put trash bags in the cans when they were back in place and didn't tell anyone or say anything to the residents.

When I came back the next day, the trash cans were overflowing with trash, and nearly all the trash on the ground had been picked up. I had citizens asking me when they put the cans in. I went to the captain of the police department, and I said, "You have been here a long time, right, sir?"

He agreed.

I asked him, "How many trash cans are in Davisville?"

He said, "None."

I asked him to really think about it. He paused for a minute and said again, "None."

I showed him before and after pictures, and he just laughed. So for around five bucks, a problem was solved. But again, there was no driving fast or running or fighting or any of the exciting police stuff. Just taking care of problems.

So if police chiefs know that officers don't want or like to do these things, why do they tell the public that they are going to do community things when they get in office? Because they know that the community want to have a say-so in what the police are doing and want to be a part of the solution when it comes to fixing a troubled community.

We, as the public, must hold our chiefs of police and the governing boards that are hiring them to the standards that they are promising us. If a chief tells us that he or she is going to lead via community this or community that, then make sure they do it. Don't accept a bunch of crap excuses, like "I am trying to get adjusted." They knew what they were getting into. I guarantee they did all the adjusting prior to taking the job. They should have come in ready to hit the ground running. If not, they are ill-prepared to do the job. When they do an opening speech, they are making campaign promises. Hold them to it.

In my samples of chiefs' speeches, you will find names like Police Chief John Diaz of Seattle, Anne Kirkpatrick of Oakland, William Bratton of Los Angeles, Patrice Andrews of Morrisville, George McNeil of Somerset, William Baldwin of Torrington, and Derrick Diggs of Fort Myers. I wonder how many of them adopted the community mindset they spoke of and how many of them are still on the job as chief of police in the jurisdictions where they were so recently giving their speeches. Let's see.

- Police Chief John Diaz—DOJ's finding is that Seattle officers routinely have used excessive force. Chief John Diaz: "Time for me to go."
- Police Chief Anne Kirkpatrick—Oakland Review Agency exonerates police chief over false statements regarding ICE raid. She is still the chief but reportedly has been asked to resign.

- William Bratton—He has stayed on for a very long time, and although he was criticized for being gone traveling for personal and professional reasons too much, he left on his own after nine years.
- Patrice Andrews—He is still in place as chief and apparently doing great.
- George McNeil—He is still in place as chief and very community involved.
- William Baldwin—He is still in place but has only been the chief for a few months. Good so far.

The bottom line is that you can see from above that the chiefs don't always do what they say they are going to do. It is up to us to hold them to their words and hold their bosses to their expectations when they hire these chiefs. Every jurisdiction should take a look at their chief of police and write an acceptance speech based on how their last year has gone. If they had to write a speech based on their actions and not their promises, what would it sound like? As they say, fill one hand with promises and the other with poop and see which one fills up first. Standing by and letting our law enforcement leaders have a pass on unacceptable behavior just cannot be done anymore, and for us to believe that the behavior of any individual officer should not have been seen or stopped by one of their supervisors is absurd.

When we start holding the police administrations responsible for the actions of the individual officer, you will see this type of rogue cop behavior stop. I can tell you that there is a college-boy mentality among a lot of law enforcement officers, but I don't know anyone who is going to take part in any of this childish behavior if they know that they are all going to be held responsible, especially the supervisors. Right now, their supervisors are working off an if-I-act-like-I-don't-know-then-I-am-okay mentality, and that is complete bullshit. Police administrations at all levels have a responsibility to know what their officers are doing, and they just have to stop being lazy and get involved with the day-to-day operations of their officers.

COMMUNITY INTERACTION REVIEWS

So as a basic review of a few law enforcement agencies across the United States, I will choose a few agencies and do a very brief review and discuss what they are doing and essentially put the information out there that they are or are not putting out there for the public to see and let you decide if it is enough to quell the possibility of an upcoming growth of discomfort in the community.

I will start close to where I went to high school (Fort Myers, Florida) and look at Cape Coral, Florida. I will start with saying that I have absolute no animosity toward Cape Coral as a city, I have no friends who live there, and I don't recall playing in any high school sports. So I cannot say that I have an ax to grind against them for any reason.

I am not familiar with any person who works there, and I am typing this prior to even reviewing the information that is posted on their website, so to the chief and his or her men and women in uniform, please do not take offense to anything that may come hereafter. This is for information purposes, and I sincerely hope that this report finds that you are all making every effort possible. If not, then perhaps this will bring to light some things that perhaps can be done for the sake of the community as a whole.

2014

So let's take a look at Cape Coral, Florida, beginning with the 2014 Annual Report, as that was the first one that I could find on the website. I saw that it listed its accomplishments as Achieved or Pending. The report was well put together and a little busy for my taste, with faded photos in the background; but all in all, it was decent.

They chose to use the wording *community governance*. I wasn't quite sure how to take that use of language, so I chose to look it up. The internet defines *governance* as the act of governing or controlling. So in other words, the Cape Coral Police Department chose to use its community outreach programs as a way to "control the community?" Hmm. Maybe just an oversight or unfortunate choice of words, but let's move on.

Public Safety Advisory Committee—awesome idea. I love it. They met quarterly, and although it used to be the Chief's Advisory Committee, it now included the fire department, so that justified the name change. No mention of topics discussed in their quarterly meetings, so I couldn't speak on what topics or community concerns were addressed or even the attendance or location of meetings. So I was not sure if this was perhaps a failing effort. It started out great but failed to provide much on the level of follow-through when it came to exuding confidence in my law enforcement if I were looking to relocate to this area.

Coffee with a Cop—amazing program. I am very familiar with it. Guidelines were already in place, and it was basically a cookie-cutter program that you could pick up and run with. This program was hosted three times in twelve months. Now I was not sure if that meant it was done much more and just hosted three times or if it was just done three times. This was something that you could do weekly if you really wanted to get feedback from the public. So three times a year told me that they were doing this to be able to put it in this report and not much else.

Shop with a Cop—another great program that was conducted once a year, on December 22, and no other details were given, such as how many kids, what stores participated, etc. So I couldn't really comment further. Could be great, but I thought they really missed an opportunity to toot their own horn when it came to getting or taking credit for what they might have done.

Holiday Heroes Food Drive—the amount of food collected and the statistics provided were absolutely amazing. Hands down the best thing I had read so far. This was what I liked to read. This shows caring, effort, and an intense sense of community by the department and everyone in it. I had no idea exactly what efforts were taken by the department, but the way this was portrayed showed that they cared. This was exactly what and how things should be shown.

2015

So here we are looking at 2015, and the report chose a new wording, *community engagement.* A much better choice of words. So we started on a higher plane with Cape Coral. Good Job, Chief. Let's see where we would go from there. I wasn't impressed at all with last year's report.

Chief's Town Hall Meetings—great Idea. I think that there is no substitute for getting out and being face-to-face with citizens and putting your neck on the line and taking questions from citizens with the understanding that you may sometimes get questions that you are not ready for. This was a brilliant step in the right direction, and I applaud the chief for taking this step and going with this program. Bravo, whoever came up with this.

Coffee with a Cop and Shop with a Cop were still on the report. I loved the programs, and I loved that they were a staple from the previous years. I would still like to see them occurring more often, but I applauded the department for showing a commitment to staying engaged and staying committed to these programs.

Tweet from the Beat—what an amazing program. One I had not heard of before, but it showed forward-thinking. I would have liked to hear some of the funny stories or examples of the interactions or maybe the number of tweets exchanged. Good work.

Social media growth was evident from the report. The experimentation in social media showed that this department saw the importance of social media in reaching the public. Good work.

Outstanding progression over last year, and since I had not lived in this area in a great many years, I would assume that based on these reports, you had no low-income housing in Cape Coral, you had no subsidized housing, and everyone in Cape Coral lived well above the poverty level. I say this because there was no community engagement efforts listed in any areas such as this. If you had people such as this, surely you would have some sort of efforts listed in those areas, right?

But the US Census Bureau showed a 13 percent poverty rate in Cape Coral, Florida. I wonder if the people in poverty were making it to the Chief's Town Hall Meetings, Tweeting from the Beat, and having Coffee with a Cop. What was being done to reach the 13 percent who were in poverty?

2016

So I saw a little bit of a different feel from the report so far. In the past the reports, they started by calling the community section *governance* and then went to *engagement*, and now, it is *community outreach*. I sensed that it was showing a downturn in the acceptance of the public. As previously discussed, *community governance* implies "control," and *community engagement* implies an "agreement," but now, we have a *community outreach* that implies "to reach beyond." It might not be intended that way, but it was coming across that way. So let's move on and see where we go.

The chief maintained an open-door policy—great idea, but I am not sure why that is necessary to state. Had something occurred that made it necessary to make that public knowledge? Concerning.

More frequent town hall meetings were held this year as well as face-to-face meetings. Great, how many? Once again, this was concerning that not more care and concern was being given to the community aspect of this report.

Do the Right Thing Program, Shop with a Cop, and Fill the Boat Programs were discussed, but no pictures and no statistics to show success. Take credit for your successes. Also, it mentioned various food drives were record-breaking. The report brushed it off like it was no big deal and lead you to believe that they really didn't care much about it.

Community Outreach Coordinator? Who is that? What is that? Connecting the department and community with many needed services? What is this? Where did it come from, and most importantly, what are the services that are needed?

The attitude from the previous paragraph showed 100 percent that whoever wrote this section either didn't like the Community Outreach Coordinator, didn't think the position was worthwhile, or thought it was just a complete waste of space. If the chief read and agreed with this section, then there was a distinct degradation in the foundation of this department that needed to be addressed.

Police Athletic League was stopped in the past, and they would like to restart it again in the future. Awesome, I hope it happens.

Wow, this was an unfortunate downturn from the previous year's report. I hope the future is more positive for the citizens of Cape Coral, Florida.

2017

Community Outreach is a total of two paragraphs in this report. So I saw that the importance of this section had fallen under this chief of police. It did, however, have lots of pretty pictures. But let's see what it said.

Community Outreach administered ongoing outreach activities, coordinated with community stakeholders, and identified potential funding to support these activities.

Oh, but here were the important numbers:

- Community events: 103
- Scholarships: 3
- Person assigned to this: 1

Cape Coral, Florida, had 170,063 people listed as its population. There was one person assigned to community outreach.

One person for 170,063 citizens.

Do you, the citizens of Cape Coral, Florida, feel like this law enforcement agency is taking your community outreach seriously?

I will not go any further with the annual reports as I believe as of the time I am typing this, there is no 2018 report ready. It is only listed as a multiyear report, and that is not applicable for my purposes.

Nothing in my short and limited evaluation of Cape Coral, Florida, showed any multicultural efforts put forth by the police department. I don't know that there are any multicultural issues in Cape Coral, Florida. They is a very limited race locality, but that doesn't mean that there won't be problems.

As I started this section, I want to reiterate that I have no issue with the Cape Coral Police Department. I don't know any of the people in Cape Coral, and I have no issue with any of the employees of that police department. I will, however, say that I am alarmed by what I am reading in their annual reports. I hope that they are just poorly written report and that the actual work being done is much more impressively diverse.

City Council of Cape Coral, take a look at what is going on and what is being published and please take heed to what is happening and not happening in your jurisdiction. This is a red flag being raised up the pole. Take notice.

Let's look elsewhere, to a place I have never been and somewhere that I have absolutely no knowledge of at all. Maybe somewhere a little further west. I will look at a map and throw the virtual dart and see where it lands.

Randomly choosing a city—Warren, Ohio.

Well, I can say that Warren, Ohio, has, without a doubt, the most detailed, in-depth, and numbers-driven report that I have ever seen. But it doesn't tell me a damn thing about what they do in the community. Well, let me back up. It tells me every traffic and parking ticket they wrote in the year, every call that every officer went on, and absolutely every enforcement effort taken; but it tells me nothing about what positive efforts were taken to engage the public.

If you are a numbers person, this is a wet dream. I went through ninety pages, and my mind was numb with desire for something positive to take away from this report.

Come on, Chief, you got to look better than this. So let's look at 2012 and see what is there because 2011 was a bust.

Well, 2012 was broken down into four sections, listed by roman numerals, and still had no community engagement information at all. I was, however, able to see the internal affairs action taken against every officer that year, including the founded and unfounded complaints and the outcome of the complaints.

So I not only had no guidance on what my law enforcement agency was doing in the public if I were looking to move to Warren, Ohio, but I could see that on September 12, Patrolman David Gallagher was suspended for being intoxicated on duty, but on November 1, Sergeant Nites was terminated for being untruthful.

So come to work drunk and you'll be suspended, but tell a lie and you're fired. Wow.

Still no indication of public interaction. Lots of enforcement action, though.

Let's see what 2013 had in store for the citizens of Warren, Ohio.

The year 2013 was very limited (seventeen pages total), and there was no report for 2014, but 2015 had a much-nicer look. Let's see what that has for us.

The year 2015 had something to show. Now we are talking. The Citizen Police Academy had reportedly been in place since 2011. But this was the first mention of it. See, I knew they were doing some good out there. See, we have to get credit for the great work we are doing and let it be known. But more importantly, do more of it.

So let's see what this Citizen Police Academy did.

Three classes: January, March, and September. A total of thirty-four graduates. Okay, not a huge turnout, but that's okay. Well, there was no reason to continue on with reviewing the annual reports for Warren, Ohio. They all looked exactly the same. Stats, stats, stats, stats.

Warren, Ohio, had 40,433 citizens listed on its census. And it graduated thirty-four people from its Citizen Academy in 2015. Was that community engagement?

Data USA listed Warren, Ohio, had 34.9 percent poverty rate. What steps were being taken to reach out to those people living below the poverty level? I saw that you had officers working in the Housing Authority areas. What special projects were they working on?

I was sure they were doing something. What were they doing? If they were not doing anything, then you were missing the boat, as they say.

So let me do a few more and see if I can find a success story.

Las Cruces, New Mexico, dedicated five pages of its 2017 Annual Report to community events. There were a lot of great pictures of things that most departments were also doing. It showed officers being silly with funny hats, reading to kids, and feeding the public. There were K9 demonstrations, ribbon-cutting ceremonies, coffee with a cop, fingerprinting activity, national night out, and youth leadership camp. And it wasn't the very last thing listed in the report like it was an afterthought.

Chief Patrick Gallagher, bravo, sir. This report was amazing, and it showed your officers in a great light. It appeared that your officers were invested in the community they served and enjoyed working with the public.

But in all fairness, and as a statement of fact, I had never been to Las Cruces, New Mexico. I will review the demographics to ensure that this was not just smoke and mirrors to cover a smoldering of problems to come.

- Home of the New Mexico State University
- Poverty rate: 24 percent
- Unemployment rate: 8 percent
- Median age: 32
- Total population: 101,712
- People with Hispanic origin: 56 percent

So in all fairness, there were a great number of photographs, but there could have been some more information on how the officers were reaching out to the individual, demographically diverse neighborhoods. They have the college in the area, and I am sure they interacted with the college as well. I still thought that this was one of the best examples of an annual report that I had seen. With a few adjustments, it was exactly what I thought the public was deserving of from their police departments.

Vallejo Police Department (California)

Although difficult to do an exact duplicate evaluation of this agency because of their lack of an annual report, I was able to find a PDF that was published of all individual community engagements per year for the years 2015 to 2017. It listed what the exact engagement was, who went, what was done, and when the exact date was.

This was freaking amazing.

- 2015: 385 community engagements
- 2016: 470 community engagements
- 2017: 320 community engagements

When you go to the Vallejo, California, Police Department website, the first thing that happens is it opens a series of videos starting with the importance of the neighborhood watch and gives credit to the officer who got it all going and shows her out in the community with citizens. It shows the officer out in the community, not the captain or lieutenant who wants to steal the credit from the real hardworking men and women. Give credit where it is due. It builds morale.

This agency has some issues on the internet with shootings and citizen complaints, but guess what, it's what we do. It's the nature of the beast, and I am not justifying whether any of those situations are justified or not. I am merely saying that this agency is portraying itself as one that cares, and it is obviously one that is out in the community and at least trying to make a difference from the center of the State of California.

This department does not portray a sense of desperation or disgust toward the community. It appears to actually like to be out in the neighborhoods and interacting with the public. The photos that I was able to see showed a positive light on law enforcement, and it seemed to be a mutual feeling between all.

MEAT AND POTATOES: WHAT IS WRONG WITH LAW ENFORCEMENT IN AMERICA?

So we get to the meat and potatoes of my reason for writing this book. I was a police officer for almost twenty-two years, and I can truly say that I spent every day doing what I absolutely loved, and I never wrote a ticket or made an arrest that I didn't feel was the right thing to do.

But in turn, I got a lot of less-than-satisfactory marks on evaluations or at least got less than what I thought I should have gotten, as everyone does.

I felt like I was continually being faced with questions, both morally and personally.

1. What are you going to do?
2. You know what is right and it's not being done. Now what?
3. Do more, do more, do more, do more.

But even though I worked through several different administrations and two different departments, there were the same political and social barriers to *Doing the Right Thing*, as Spike Lee might say.

So what were the stresses and hurdles that prevented total and complete success?

Some were me, as I would learn much later, sitting in church and hearing very distinctly from Dr. Marcus Campbell. It is ungodly not to submit to your supervision at work.

But at the same time, there were governmental and political stresses in the workplace that continued to keep certain socioeconomic groups of people from truly getting a chance at a better life and fulfilling their American Dream.

While I studied and investigated to write this book, I learned a lot of the history of the decay of the institution of law enforcement in America and, at the same time, the gov-ernment's attempts to reestablish and rebuild and repair the foundations of trust needed "to insure domestic tranquility," as the preamble to the Constitution of the United States guarantees.

It is truly a sad testimony to the process by which the United States goes through about every thirty years to see a crumbling of the foundations of law enforcement and its grounds to serve the public. From the Wickersham Commission to the Kerner Commission, we see how the government has seen a systematic wariness by the public of the very men and women that we teach our children to seek when they are in need, to seeing those same men and women demonized on the nightly news because of sex crimes and physical assaults to shootings of unarmed people of any race different than theirs.

So what is wrong with law enforcement in America?

We are getting off base from the core principles of what we swear to do.

We put on the uniform, vest, gun, and badge every day, swearing to go out and make a difference. But somewhere along the lines, we are losing or have lost track of just what difference we are supposed to be making.

We are being stressed with governmental requirements to present numbers to justify the large sums of money that we require in order to fight crime effectively because as you may or may not know, without money, you cannot possi-bly fight crime.

Crime is Money

Throughout history, we are forever looking for a better, more efficient mousetrap. What's the best way to catch the criminal? And everyone wants to be the guy who figured it out. I use *guy* interchangeably to mean all people in this instance. But it has to be an easy-to-recognize, easy-to-explain, and easy-to-claim system that can be sold to the next agency, and Chief John Doe can hang his hat on it as he prepares for retirement.

Well, guess what, there is no better, faster mousetrap.

Old faithful is the only tried and true manner in solving crimes and catching the bad guy, but it doesn't allow anyone to get famous and have a reason to be remembered as they fade off into the oblivion once they retire.

If you review the chapter on the new chiefs' speeches, you will find many similarities in what they claim they are going to do as they take over as chief or finally take the title of chief.

Most glaringly, none of those speeches say, "Thank you for making me chief of police. We are going to work hard on doing as many search warrants as possible, sting operations to arrest prostitutes, and long hours preparing apologies for the police shootings we will have in my tenure as your chief of police."

What they do say is that "We are going to work together as a community, and we are going to listen to your concerns and work together to create a stronger town to raise a family."

But in almost every one of these occasions, if you go back to the same agencies a year, two years, or even five years later, you will find some similar things.

Oftentimes, the chief is no longer employed there, crime is either the same or worse, and none of the promises made regarding working together with the community were upheld.

The studies conducted in the thirties and again the late sixties and early seventies indicated that many of the problems in the departments with increasing crime rates were those that had police chiefs that stayed less than five years, and the studies focused on the importance of crime prevention strategies.

But very few departments spend any time or effort on crime prevention.

In my tenure with the two police departments, I became certified as a crime prevention officer. But I had to do all the legwork on this and had to constantly fight with my sergeant, captain, and major in order to get a simple signature from the chief of police acknowledging that I had completed the state requirements in order to be certified.

Once I received the acknowledgment of my certification, I was never recognized by the department for this accomplishment. I was just told I didn't give them a chance to do so. I still don't understand that line of thinking. Jealousy, I suppose.

I truly believe that the reason for this is that crime prevention hurts the bottom line. Remember that crime is money, so how do we keep doing what we do while effectively reducing and preventing crimes?

We had a complete block party in several places around town, which is a story for later on in the book.

The greatest compliment I ever received as a police officer was from a gentleman whose name I wish I could recall so I could give him credit for this. He said, "Johnson, I like you. You never fucked with no one didn't need fucking with."

And that was true. People knew me and knew that if I came around and you weren't doing anything wrong, then there was no reason to run or act crazy. But if you did act funny, you were going to see me up close and personal.

We have to know our communities and not just when we're going on calls for service or going to a neighborhood watch meeting at someone's house or a local church.

We need to really know these neighborhoods. Get out and rake leaves for the elderly woman on the corner when you see that she is struggling. Help someone carry in groceries when they are unloading.

Not all the time, but every now and then. Go to neighborhood watch meetings at work and at home. Really care about the concerns that people have and try to do something about them.

Okay, here it comes, the real hard part about fixing the problem.

Talk to people face-to-face, not on the phone, if at all possible, and respond to the concerns that people have.

Notice I said *respond* to the concerns?

There are going to be issues that you can't fix. If that is the fact in whatever topic you have been asked to address, then be honest and say, "I cannot fix that."

But be able to explain why you cannot do it or show what efforts you made in order to attempt to address this issue unsuccessfully.

The average person does not expect the police to solve all the world's problems that they want some sort of relief to the problem for which they called you.

But the real problem with fixing the issues in most neighborhoods is not gaining the trust of the communities because that can be done by any officer willing to put in his or her time and really listen to the problems. It's not getting officers to sign up to take the job to become a law enforcement officer because there are thousands upon thousands of us that have had law enforcement in our bloods from the time we were in kindergarten and drawing a cartoon drawing of what we wanted to do when we grow up, as in my case. The problem lies in where you have police administrations who are facing the ends of their careers and have not seen any real significant change in crime rates since they first put on the badge, shield, or whatever they like to refer to it as, and are now faced with a subordinate officer or deputy that comes to them and says, "I can fix it."

The first instinct of most law enforcement administrations is to laugh, completely ignore them, or in most cases, give it no attention whatsoever. But as I showed in my twenty-two years in law enforcement, I could fix it. But it took a very unique set of circumstances and, what I would come to find out, an executive director of public housing with what I believed to be an unprecedented level of faith and trust in both me and a young attorney who had been born and raised in the same public housing areas that we were now patrolling.

So let's start this part of the story in 1999, and I am working in Hopewell, a small blue-collar town on the East Coast of the United States, and it is often known by commercial airline pilots as the point on the East Coast  where they prepare their descent into Washington, DC, due to the smoke from the chemical plants coming up into the air being so colorful and thick that it transcends any and all weather patterns.

I started in Hopewell at the end of 1999 and almost immediately found out that there was going to be a specialty assignment in the public housing areas for an officer to have. Well, coming from Petersburg Police, where I worked on the Weed and Seed Program, which was a federal grant program to fight drugs and reestablish communities, I was familiar with what I believed to be the needs of the assignment in public housing and was anxious to jump into that assignment. I found out that no one wanted the assignment in public housing, and it would be forced on someone if no one put in for it. Since I was new to the Hopewell Police Department but not new to police work, I decided to put in for it.

After meeting with Chief Wayne Cleveland and interviewing for the position, I was given the position, and I was to start working approximately a month later. In my preparation for the assignment, I started spending as much time as possible in these housing areas to see what I had gotten myself into, so I spoke to the maintenance workers, residents, and mailmen. I found many things to be true and similar in the days that led up to being assigned to the Hopewell Housing Authority for two and a half years. The properties were run-down, dirty, and nothing to be proud of.

So I went to Mr. Martin Blaney, who was the executive director of the Hopewell Redevelopment and Housing Authority, and asked him, "What is it you want me to accomplish while I am assigned to HRHA?"

His response to me was "Make people responsible for themselves, proud of where they live, and reduce crime in public housing."

I thought, *Well, okay, shouldn't be too hard.* But if you looked at what I found to be commonplace in all the housing areas, it was in direct conflict with what Mr. Blaney wanted from me at this point in our juncture.

I spoke with the maintenance workers in public housing, and they were just completely overworked, underpaid, underappreciated, and under facilitated. So how do you fix it? I took it to the board. My first official day with the Housing Authority, I was to join Mr.

Blaney at an executive board meeting to be introduced to the board. Just prior to going into the meeting, I asked if I could speak to the board. He agreed and I spoke.

"Good evening, ladies and gentlemen, I am Officer Kevin Johnson of the Hopewell Police Department. I have been a police officer for five years, and I come from the Petersburg Police Department where I have been assigned to the Weed and Seed Program for approximately the last six months. I am excited to get started with the Hopewell Redevelopment and Housing Authority, and if I could for just a minute, I would like to tell you just a few things that I have noticed as I drive around the housing areas in Hopewell. I noticed that the properties are in need of maintenance, grass cutting, and overall cleaning. Now it is important to note that it is not the fault of the maintenance department as I have spoken to them, and they are working extremely hard to get their jobs done, but they are just overworked and stressed. They cannot do it with the current staff that they have. On top of doing the day-to-day maintenance, they have to cut the grass, trim trees, and weed eat the properties. Well, that is just too much to ask. I was asked to get the residents to show some pride in their communities, and to tell you the truth, I just don't see anything worth being proud of. I look forward to working together with everyone, and I hope that we can make a difference with all this."

As a result of this meeting, the executive board ended up hiring a contractor to do all the grass cutting, tree trimming, and weed eating, and added additional maintenance staff to fill positions that had been vacant.

I then met with a young property manager, named Bridgette Hopson, who happened to have her juris doctorate in law. She was a bright-eyed young African American female who had been raised in these same public housing areas and had made it out but kept her promise to always remember where she came from and always make a difference. (She still does to this day.)

Bridgette and I were like brothers and sisters separated at birth but from different racially based families. We saw eye to eye on most things and could discuss and hash out any problem and come to a solution. I had always said she was a godsend to the Hopewell Redevelopment and Housing Authority.

I shared my ideas of how I wanted to deal with the public and effectively deal with problems. Bridgette shared her experiences as well, and we had a great working relationship.

Here is a statement that I will make that a lot of people will disagree with, but if done correctly, it is the truth. Public housing is easily fixable if done correctly, and you can greatly enhance the lives of the people who live there. Yes, I said "easily fixable." That doesn't mean that it is easy to obtain the end result. It just means that the process by which you must go about change to gain the end result is easy.

What it takes in order to fix public housing are a few basic, easy steps, and if taken early and in an exacting manner, you, too, can obtain the 74 percent drop in crime that we—my partner, Officer Harry Mars, and I—obtained in Hopewell in two and a half years. We were able to obtain this by making very few arrests and writing very few summonses but through the courts and eviction of scores of people.

Before anyone would move into any housing area, there must be a lease agreement. Look over the lease agreement and ensure that there are several things in the lease.

Acknowledgment of understanding and responsibility for the following:

- a. Property
- b. Trash
- c. Guests
- d. Rent
- e. Zero tolerance for law violations
- f. Vehicle parking violations and removal
- g. Payment of utilities (if applicable)
- h. Subleasing absolutely denied
- i. Drug violations will result in lifetime ban from all housing areas in all fifty states, whether you are arrested or not

j. Lease violation notices (three strikes and your eviction process starts)

k. Only blood relatives and married people may live together in housing and must be on the lease

Lease violation notices can be issued by any law enforcement officer assigned to public housing or working for public housing or any employee of the public housing agency. The paperwork process starts in order to show a pattern of noncompliance with the standards of the Housing Authority.

I learned long ago not to reinvent the wheel. I searched the internet early in my assignment and found what other people assigned to public housing were doing and catered it to my assignment, and I was never too proud to share that with anyone else. But you will see in law enforcement that there is a fundamental difference with many people. Oftentimes, law enforcement middle management will never share credit or blame. If it is your idea, then it is ridiculous and can't be worthwhile. But if it is your idea and it is failing, then they are ready to pounce and to write you up.

Just knowing that keeps many great law enforcement officers from really becoming all that they truly can be in the career that they have sought their entire lives to be a part of.

The very leaders in law enforcement that are supposed to be guiding and directing the young officers to lead and direct our future oftentimes will stand by in wait, like a jungle cat waiting to pounce at the first sign of adversity in any program that you may be assigned to that is showing prosperity.

Such as the HRHA assignment. Officer Mars and I had arranged for a few community festivals over the years, from back to school to end of school, to winter coat drives, and we had gradually included the community more and more in the planning and implementation process. Quite honestly, never knowing if they would catch on in the planning process, we were always prepared to take over if necessary. They always succeeded beyond our wildest dreams.

During one particular festival, we were having a summer festival, and it was going great. I recall there was softball, horseshoes, hot dogs on the grill, a DJ, basketball, etc. I called the captain, who happened to be working, who I will say is Captain Jay for identifications sake, and said, "Hey, sir, we are having a festival down in Davisville. I wondered if you could come over and walk around for a while."

I got the typical response, "Why, what's wrong?"

"Nothing, sir, I just think it would do some good to let people see some of the administration walking around the festival and showing support."

"Did you call the patrol sergeant?"

"Yes, sir."

"Okay, well, if they should be able to handle it, if anything goes wrong, let me know."

Needless to say, I never saw the captain or the sergeant. A few of the residents of Davisville heard my phone conversation and came to me later and said, "You didn't really think they were coming out here, did you?"

I never spoke publicly against the administration, but this was one time that it was difficult. This is the perception of the public. And as we know, perception is reality whether we like it or not. All it would have taken was for the captain to come over and walk around for even a minute or two and show that the citizens in public housing were important, and it could have started to change the perception. He was in the office at the headquarters, which was maybe a half a mile as the crow flies from where I was having the festival.

But the lack of response and the lack of simple effort by the captain was displayed in the trickle-down effect to the patrol sergeant who also didn't show up. Now let me lay to rest some people's excuses that perhaps the captain and sergeant were busy and couldn't make it. One simple word—no. Not too busy. Just didn't care. It took the police department to care in order to get the same response out of the public.

As a matter of fact, the logo that used to be on the cars for the police department in Hopewell was "We Care," and after much complaining by the officers, they had it removed. What message does that deliver? It used to be a joke that "We Used to Care" or "We No Longer Care." So now there was no logo on the cars. What message does that send?

As we move to the statistical review portion of this section, I found a very interesting quote from an article I was reading relating to how law enforcement administrators have tried to mold their current style of policing into community policing for the purposes of grant funding. Remember this quote as we move forward and see where it was done.

Community Policing: Promise
and Failure (May 15, 2015)

Perhaps the most well-known version of bastard-ized community policing—stop-and-frisk—has not only alienated entire communities but has proven completely ineffective as a blunt-force crime-fighting strategy as well. [Watch for the yellow highlighter.]

So let's review, as everyone should, the goals and accomplishments of their individual department's community efforts. What do they say about the growth and advancement of your police department or law enforcement agency? Most agencies post this information on the web for all to see. After all, they are proud of it. Let's use Hopewell as an example.

For the year 2011, these were what we did:

- Engaging the community
    - Conducted six command walks to include the following (in twelve months, one every other month):
        - The Heights
        - Vanguard
        - Piper Square
        - City Point
        - Beat 312
        - Fifteenth Street Business Corridor Christmas walk
    - Conducted twenty outdoor roll calls. (*Outdoor roll call* is defined as standing at an intersection as the morning information is provided to the officers prior to starting their workday.)
    - Attended numerous school functions and Hopewell social events (such as—).
    - Attended citywide neighborhood watch (one per month in city council chambers).
    - Attended individual neighborhood watch meetings. (That was my job.)
    - Attended Ward Town Hall Meetings. (This happened very infrequently, if at all.)
    - Helped establish a tri-city homicide family support group. (We were most likely asked to be a part of this.)

So these were the momentous efforts that the City of Hopewell were undertaking in order to engage the community. And these were what they were bragging about in their annual report to the mayor, city Manager, and the public. Yet there was no public outrage.

Let's move to 2012 and see if things got any better.

- Engaging the community
    - Conducted eight command walks (an increase of two over last year, which is a little better.)

- ○ Conducted 127 outdoor roll calls (an increase of 107 over last year, which is impressive).
- ○ Engaged the faith leaders
- ○ Formed partnership with OC3 faith leaders. (This was in place but poorly attended by the admin.)
- ○ Reestablish the TRIAD program to reduce crime against the elderly. Launch date was set for May 2013. (Launch set for 2013? Why was it on this report?)
- ○ Created the department Facebook page, with over 1,600 likes, to inform the community. (My idea, and I had to fight for it.)

So these were the momentous efforts that the City of Hopewell were undertaking in order to engage the community. And these were what they were bragging about in their annual report to the mayor, city manager, and the public. Yet there was no public outrage.

Let's move to 2013 and see if things got any better.

- • Engaging the community
  - ○ No mention of command walks? What happened?
  - ○ Conducted 175 outdoor roll calls (increase of almost 50, looking good.)
  - ○ Conducted 1,766 field interviews: a 2 percent increase from 2012. (Are field interviews community engagement? FIs, as we called them, are usually done on suspects.)
  - ○ Held the First Annual Police Activities League (PAL) Summer Camp: thirty children attended (awesome, my idea).
  - ○ Conducted Gang Awareness and Prevention Forum: 120 in attendance (1 class, 1 day, but good stuff).
  - ○ Conducted Gang Prevention Forums for all high school and middle school students (one class, one day, but good stuff).

o   Conducted 1,543 hours of alternative patrols—foot and bike patrol. (Are patrols engagement or enforcement? Okay, I'll take it.)

o   Held a National Night Out: 15 neighborhoods and 1,500 citizens participated, with a visit from the governor and secretary of public safety at the Kippax Neighborhood Watch event. (This was 1 night but usually a great event hated by most officers.)

o   Conducted Gang Awareness Training for Hopewell Public School employees. (Same as above? Maybe I'll take it.)

So these were the momentous efforts that the City of Hopewell were undertaking in order to engage the community. And these were what they were bragging about in their annual report to the mayor, city manager, and the public. Yet there was no public outrage.

Let's move to 2014 and see if things got any better

• Engaging the community
    o   Attended Hopewell Community Day with Virginia Attorney General Mark Herring: 250 attended. (It was a great event. I was recognized by the attorney general. Oh, that inflamed the administration.)

    o   Held the Second Annual Hopewell Police Summer Camp: 75 children attended (awesome, my idea).

    o   Held a Police Explorers Bike Rodeo: 80 children attended (awesome program).

    o   Conducted 210 outdoor roll calls (an increase of 35, bravo).

    o   Conducted 1,766 field interviews: a 2 percent increase from 2013. (Are field interviews community engagement? FIs, as we called them, are usually done on suspects.)

    o   Held Gang Prevention Forums for all high school and middle school students. (Good idea, I will take it.)

- ○ Conducted 2,025 hours of alternative patrols—foot and bike patrol: 24 percent increase from 2013. (Still feeling like this is enforcement, not engagement. I think they are missing the point of community engagement.)
- ○ Held a National Night Out: 8 neighborhoods and 1,500 citizens participated. (This was 1 night but usually a great event hated by most officers, but wait, 8 neighborhoods? It was 15 last year. What happened?)

So these were the momentous efforts that the City of Hopewell were undertaking in order to engage the community. And these were what they were bragging about in their annual report to the mayor, city manager, and the public. Yet there was no public outrage.

Let's move to 2015 and see if things got any better.

- • Engaging the community
  - ○ Purchased, trained, and implemented Body Worn Camera Project. (Why is this community engagement?)
  - ○ Delivered over five hundred cases of water to seniors and shut-ins due to the water emergency. (Okay, I will take it. FYI, overtime was charged to the water company.)
  - ○ Held the Hopewell Crime and Gang Summit: ninety citizens and city leaders in attendance. (I was acknowledged by the community, which enflamed the administration.)
  - ○ Held the John Randolph Foundation / City of Hopewell Youth Day: four hundred attended. (I have no memory of this, but okay.)
  - ○ Held the Third Annual Hopewell Police Summer Camp: ninety-five children attended. (Awesome, I was reprimanded for too many kids.)

- ○ Held a Bike Rodeo and Safety Day: sixty children attended (another amazing effort).
- ○ Attended the Third Annual Homicide Support Group Holiday Vigil. (We were invited, so I'm not sure how we take credit for this.)
- ○ Held a National Night Out: ten neighborhoods participated. (This was one night but usually a great event hated by most officers. Ten neighborhoods? Up from eight.)
- ○ Held a Patrol Holiday Food Drive: 1,500 pounds of food collected and over 1,000 positive citizen contacts. (1,000? Okay.)
- ○ Held a Patrol "Candy Cane from Cops" Holiday Initiative: 2,117 positive contacts with candy canes and holiday safety tips. (My program, and I was ridiculed by many for handing out candy canes with crime prevention tips attached.)
- ○ Gave ninety-one wrapped gifts to children. (Another one of mine, and the gifts were donated by 7-Eleven and Dollar General.)
- ○ Conducted 308 outdoor roll calls (An increase of almost 100. But now the admin no longer attended.)
- ○ Conducted six command walks or reset in neighborhoods. (Command walks are back, six a year.)
- ○ Conducted 1,642 field interviews (almost 4.5 people a day were being stopped by the police just to talk—engagement or harassment?)
- ○ Maintained Facebook: 2,854 followers. (Awesome, they are finally believers.)

So these were the momentous efforts that the City of Hopewell were undertaking in order to engage the community. And these were what they were bragging about in their annual report to the mayor, city manager, and the public. Yet there was no public outrage.

Let's move to 2016 and see if things got any better. My final year.

- Engaging the community or community policing efforts
  - Implemented fully the Body Worn Camera Project in 2016. (I still don't see how this is community engagement.)
  - Held the Fourth Annual Hopewell Police Summer Camp: sixty children attended. (Awesome and taken over now that it's a good idea.)
  - Participated in HEROS camp with Hopewell Recreation and Parks (ran by Parks and Rec, great thing).
  - Attended the Fourth Annual Homicide Support Group Holiday Vigil. (We attended, good thing.)
  - Attended the Community Prayer and Forum at Carter G. Woodson. (We attended, good thing.)
  - Held a National Night Out: nine neighborhoods participated. (This was one night but usually a great event hated by most officers. Nine neighborhoods? Down from ten.)
  - Held a Career Days at Carter G. Woodson and Harry E. James. (Okay, good thing.)
  - Held a school painting project at DuPont Elementary. (During the summer, a few officers helped paint an empty school, but I'm not sure that was engaging the community.)
  - Held a Patrol Holiday Food Drive: 500 pounds of food collected and over 325 positive citizen contacts (awesome).
  - Held a Patrol "Candy Cane from Cops" Holiday Initiative: 2,117 positive contacts with candy canes and holiday safety tips. (My program, and I was ridiculed by many for handing out candy canes with crime prevention tips attached.)

o Gave ninety-one wrapped gifts to children. (Another one of mine, and the gifts were donated by 7-Eleven and Dollar General.)

o Conducted 230 outdoor roll calls. (Down almost 80 from lasts year. Admin still did not attend.)

o Held nine command walks or reset in neighborhoods. (Command walks were back and on the increase. Great.)

o Participated in the Annual DEA Drug Takeback Event where Hopewell Police Department collected and delivered 105.7 pounds of medication to the DEA area office. (Great program.)

o Conducted 962 field interviews. (That was 2.6 people being stopped and talked to a day. Still seemed like harassment.)

o Grew Facebook: 2,854 followers (awesome).

o Handed out 600 Cop-sicles or freeze pops to children at HRHA properties. (After an officer gave out of pocket to start this, the department got on board and helped out. Good job.)

o Held an Easter egg Hunt: gave 135 filled eggs to children in Davisville and Bland Court (awesome).

o Visited elementary schools weekly for Lunch with Cops (awesome).

o Participated in Special Olympics Torch Run. (Only law enforcement could run. How was this community engagement?)

o Joined the Jogs 4 Dogs Adoption and Fundraising Event where the Animal Control coordinated with HHS track team (awesome).

o Joined the Animal Control Stars for Paws Adoption program (awesome).

o Held a Courthouse Road Community Cleanup (awesome).

o Held the Education Fantasy League for DuPont Elementary where HPD served as mentors or coaches for three fourth grade teams. (Never heard of this, but I will take it. Awesome!)

So things are definitely getting better for the City of Hopewell at the way we are engaging the community. I think that there are disconnects between what community engagement means compared to community entanglement. Just because you have come in contact with someone in public doesn't mean you have engaged that person positively.

In order to promote positive change for the future, you must positively engage the public, not have community entanglements. Field interviews are almost exclusively community entanglements, and yet the City is proud of them and brags of them yearly in their annual report.

Let's move to 2017 and see how we rounded this out as of the time I am writing this book.

- Community engagement or community policing (snapshot)
    - Held the Fifth Annual Hopewell Police Summer Camp: sixty children attended. (Awesome! Great to see this still going.)
    - Participated in HEROS camp with Hopewell Recreation and Parks. (Awesome! Great to see this still going.)
    - Attended the Fifth Annual Homicide Support Group Holiday Vigil. (Again, we were invited, but great program).
    - Held the First Church Safety and Awareness Forum: fifteen churches were represented. (Great program. Good Stuff.)
    - Conducted the Second Annual HPD Blood Drive. (No mention of this last year. But good stuff.)
    - Held a National Night Out: nine neighborhoods participated. (Awesome, always a great way to engage the community.)
    - Held a Career Days at Hopewell High School, Carter G. Woodson, and Harry E. James. (Good stuff.)

o Held a Lunch with a Cop at elementary schools: forty visits (Forty? Really? Okay.)

o Held the Second Annual Big Brother or Big Sisters Bowling Fundraiser: $3,000 donated by HPD. (This should be $3,000 raised by HPD. Good job.)

o Held a Patrol Holiday Food Drive: 750 pounds of food collected and over 400 positive citizen contacts (awesome).

o Held a Patrol "Candy Cane from Cops" Holiday Initiative: over two thousand positive contacts with candy canes and holiday safety tips. (My program, and I was ridiculed by many for handing out candy canes with crime prevention tips attached.)

o Held the DEA Drug Takeback: two collection events collected over 250 pounds of unused medication (great).

o Conducted the TRIAD: five meetings to improve the quality of life and crime prevention for seniors. (Triad is a sheriff's program.)

o Donated five new bikes for the Harry E. James Elementary Good Conduct Award (awesome).

o Grew Facebook: 4,100 followers (amazing).

o Handed out 600 Cop-sicles or freeze pops to children at HRHA properties (amazing).

o Joined the Jogs 4 Dogs Adoption or Fundraising Event where the Animal Control coordinated with HHS track team (amazing).

o Served as mentors or coaches for three fourth grade education teams at DuPont Elementary School (amazing).

o Conducted 260 outdoor roll calls. (An increase of 30 over last year. Good job.)

o Conducted twelve command walks or reset in neighborhoods. (Twelve. Good job. Once a month.)

o Conducted 848 field interviews. (There were 2.3 people a day being stopped and interviewed. Still doesn't sit well with me.) Remember the quote I copied in the beginning of this section? It said that things like these field interviews had been proven completely ineffective.

So as a whole, where do we stand as a city? I think that it shows that there were some efforts being taken to remain active within the community, but there were very little efforts being taken outside of the schools and existing programs to actually engage the public.

Where were the faith-based communities being fostered? Where were the efforts to engage the youth that didn't go to summer camp? It didn't mention that the summer camp, after it was taken away from me, was moved to a nicer public park and the number of attendees was limited and selective. Selective meant that when the notices were sent home in the elementary schools, the cut off had already been met, and the kids that wanted to go couldn't anyway.

That was when the selected members of society made a call to the right person or the friend of the friend had a slot held for them in the summer camp. I held my camp in the back of a school yard where most of the kids that really needed interaction with the police could walk or the parents without vehicles could walk them to camp.

That was the interaction that I fostered as the community relations officer and the type of relationship that you must build within your community in order to prevent an unnecessary development of anger and tension between the public and the police.

But that was exactly the relationship that the administration that came up as Captain Johnny B. Goode wasn't comfortable with.

Here is a quick test. Stop a law enforcement officer and ask him what his first name is. See if he answers it. If not, ask him why he doesn't answer it. Don't be aggressive. I know of no department anywhere that restricts the use of anyone's first name. No one is named Officer. At least I have never seen a birth certificate with the first name of Officer. I have seen Judge and Sir. But never Officer.

Anyone really comfortable with their connection with the community will offer their first name in a conversation with the public. Now that doesn't mean that you should use their first name when speaking to them. You probably don't know them, and that would be disrespectful. But if they will not tell you their first name, they cannot honestly tell you that they are comfortable with the public. It's public information. We can get it.

So let's discuss public housing for a few minutes.

Public housing was established to provide decent and safe rental housing for eligible low-income families, the elderly, and persons with disabilities.

Housing Authorities will deny admission to any applicant whose habits and practices may be expected to have a detrimental effect on other tenants or on the project's environment.

What is the role of the housing authority?

1. Ongoing functions:
   a. Assure compliance with leases
   b. Set other charges (e.g., security deposit, excess utility consumption, and damages to unit)
   c. Perform periodic reexaminations of the family's income at least once every twelve months
   d. Transfer families from one unit to another, in order to correct over/under crowding, to repair or renovate a dwelling, or to grant a resident's request to be transferred
   e. Terminate leases when necessary
   f. Maintain the development in a decent, safe, and sanitary condition

Once you begin to establish a pattern of noncompliance with the standards set forth in the lease, you keep the paperwork, and after the set number of violations to the lease, you send notification to the lease holder that the process has begun to have their lease terminated and the eviction process will begin. And as I used to tell people, they would be receiving their invitation.

Invitation to live somewhere else.

Once a person is evicted, make sure that their belongings are removed either by them or by the local authorities. If that person is to reapply for public housing, ensure that they are either put back on the bottom of the waiting list or, based on the reason that they are evicted, have a mandatory time period that they must wait before reapplying.

You must not allow exceptions to the eviction rules without specific reasons for exception or you will be setting yourself up for lawsuits.

This process is not hard, it is not lengthy, but it takes time, and it takes cooperation between the local law enforcement agency assigned to the Housing Authority and the housing manager, and especially the courts who handle the evictions. I fully expect the local courts to be overwhelmed when these cases start rolling in, but after the first wave of evictions come and go, they will slow to an almost trickle, and the housing crimes will drop for fear of being evicted.

Anyone in common areas of public housing must be either a tenant or in the company of a tenant or will otherwise be considered trespassing.

This cannot be stressed enough. In almost 90 percent of cases of drugs and violence in public housing, the perpetrators do not live legally in public housing. They are usually staying with someone. So if they are approached by the police in public housing and are not with a tenant, they are trespassing and can be arrested.

If they are with a tenant, then any illegal activity that they are undertaking will be attributed to the tenant and can therefore result in their eviction.

Anyone seen running from a common area and hiding or running into an apartment will result in the blame being on the tenant, who is the lease holder for the apartment, and can therefore result in the eviction of that tenant.

Yearly Health and Welfare Inspections

There must be yearly health and welfare inspections of all the apartments, and there must be consequences for the failed inspections. I realize that most people think that if they fail, they can just violate the lease and put them out, but I know that is not the case. Teach the housekeeping classes, inspect, inspect, inspect, then start the eviction process.

(f) Maintain the development in a decent, safe, and sanitary condition.

Remember, this is in the guidelines for HUD. All people are entitled to a decent, safe, and sanitary condition, and that means that the people that live around them must be held to that standard.

I lived in public housing for five years while I was a police officer, and I have many fond memories of my years in Thomas Rolfe Court, Hopewell, Virginia. There were consequences for the tenants, and on only two occasions can I remember having to take any police action when I was off duty. I respected the other residents, and I feel like they respected me as well. My family lived with me there, and they never had any problems.

The way to fix public housing is to address it as you would address any out-of-control issue involving human beings. Get back to the root of the problem, set goals and standards, maintain those goals and standards, be consistent, and follow through with what you say.

Rules are meant to be acted upon accordingly. Soft rules result in disorganization, much like you see housing areas nowadays.

Empty Promises, Empty Threats

Here are two things I heard so often out of dealing with communities of any kind:

1. We should do a community event of some kind
2. Those cameras are going to get you arrested

If you're not going to do a community event or sit down and plan one on a specific date and actually make it happen, don't talk about it. Empty promises do more harm than good. Don't look for accolades for your community events, especially not the first two or ten that you do. That will come later when you least expect it.

Cameras are great to deter crimes from the people who are looking for a new place to start doing crimes or for people that are not used to committing crimes. Most career criminals know that your bullshit cameras aren't going to do a damn thing to stop anything they are doing. Your government-funded housing project can't afford a camera system that is good enough to be able to identify the person, place, or thing that is going on, so your empty threat becomes a joke in the neighborhood, and you look completely incompetent when you make the threat.

Or in my case, you have maintenance people who go in at some point in the evening or night and point all the cameras at the ground, so if I tried to look at what happened, all I could see was the ground anyway.

Cameras are for honest people and are a tool to help you establish a basic understanding of who, what, where, when and why, not exactly who, what, where, when, and why. I never once made a case based on any camera footage.

Come as You Are

Come to work sometimes in plain clothes and just be around. Hang out and sit around the areas that people like to sit around. People-watch. Take pictures with an old camera that has no film in it. Keep people guessing. Come in during evening hours in the summer wearing a police uniform with shorts and hang out and see who is barbecuing and buy chips or napkins and just drop them off and leave, even if not asked. Be in the community and play with the kids. I used to go to Walmart, Kmart, or the Dollar Store and buy sporting goods as cheap as possible and keep them in the trunk of my police car. I would drive around anywhere in town, and if I saw kids outside playing, I would stop and get some of the sporting goods out of my trunk and then drive back by and throw the ball out of my car at the kids and just keep driving. If I got a chance, I would stop by later and see if they were still outside. If so, I would stop and play with them or talk for a few minutes. It didn't matter that I gave them the ball. It mattered that a police officer gave them a ball.

Believe me, kids know you, know your car number, know your name, know what you drive off duty, know if your married, know if you have kids, know if you have a dog, know if you have a motorcycle, etc. Think I am lying? Stop and ask someone and see what they know. If they don't know you, consider yourself a failure.

A police officer's job is to help the community. If you are not engaged with the community, then you cannot help the community. You cannot just drive around every day and wait for a call to see if someone needs help. When I was assigned to public housing, I used to have to tell people that if there was a problem, please call the police. They wanted to deal with only me or my partner Harry, affectionately known as Black Cop. He is African American, and I am Caucasian. It was Johnson and Black Cop or Project Cops.

We were known by the residents as the ones that they could depend on and would do all we could to help them, but if there was nothing we could do, we would just tell you up front, "There isn't anything I can do." People want the truth, but more importantly, they want a public servant who cares and is compassionate about what they are going through.

So with that said, what is wrong with the police today? Why are we seeing more and more civil disobedience and civil disruption?

I have what I believe to be an interesting theory on this.

Police officers have the job that fifty years ago the cool kids didn't want. The cool kids went on to be army rangers, Hollywood stars, stuntmen, or some other macho-type job. The nice guy who wasn't really the popular kid in school went on to be the local police officer. He was the guy who didn't necessarily go away to college but maybe stayed home and went to community college or was a volunteer fire fighter on the weekends. Maybe he was in the National Guard for one weekend a month and two weeks in the summer.

So John Q. Public was Mr. Dependable and worked in your dad's hardware store in the 1950s, knew everyone in town, and played baseball in high school but wasn't the high school quarterback. Did I paint a good enough picture?

So while the macho popular guys were off changing the world being politicians or sports stars or whatever they were doing, the dependable guys like me were patrolling the streets and doing the grunt work of keeping the hometowns safe and sound for Johnny B. Goode to come home to a popularity parade once in a while.

Well, recessions came and went, and national tragedies came and went, and we were involved in several wars, and all of a sudden, our macho men became more and more associated with guns and defending the homeland.

We saw people becoming more affectionate toward our lawmen with the likes of people from these shows:

- *Dragnet* (1951)
- *The Andy Griffith Show* (1960)
- *Columbo* (1968)
- *CHiPs* (1977)
- *Hill Street Blues* (1981)

But if you notice with each of the examples above, none of them are very flashy, with the possible exception of *CHiPs*, in the late seventies. But that would indicate the change in the tide for law enforcement and possibly when the next indication of decay in our law enforcement community began.

Our society was experiencing a systematic change in the way we were bringing in money. We were having husbands and wives that were both working, and Hollywood was raising our kids, and we started seeing police officers and detectives on the screens in our living rooms, and they were doing cool things like kicking peoples doors in and chasing people around in fast cars.

All of a sudden, the lines between the faithful old guy in high school and the superstar high school quarterback were becoming blurred. But we were losing sight of why the faithful old guy became the police officer in the first place.

He was the guy everyone knew. He was the guy who passed the background check without an FBI fingerprint scan because he had always been around and couldn't possibly be involved in anything bad. He was trustworthy. You took his word because he had always been a man of his word. If your daughter brought him home, you would be proud to have him as your son-in-law. Yeah, he knew about high-speed chases and kicking in doors, but he never had to do them because he didn't have to do them. No one ran from him because he knew who they were and wouldn't get away with it anyway. He didn't kick the door in because if he had to get the door open, he knew where you kept the spare key.

But that's not what they did on TV. Your job must be so cool. So now Johnny B. Goode moves back home after a failed attempt at politics or Hollywood or whatever he did out West, and he is back in his home town, and he is used to being the big man on campus, and everyone loves him. Well, now he has been away for years, and the younger generations don't know who he is and truthfully don't really care who he is.

So Johnny B. Goode comes back home and still knows the mayor. He needs a job, and the mayor makes him a police officer. Back when Johnny was in elementary school, he was a little bit of a bully, and it got him what he wanted, and everyone thought he was cool. So he keeps on doing it, but he now does it with his coworkers and the citizens who don't know him because after all, he is Johnny B. Goode. Everyone knows he is the coolest of the cool.

But the faithful old officer has set the precedent for police officers in this area, so Johnny gets the same respect as everyone else because of the foundation that has been set, but now things are starting to change. We are starting to see the crumbling of the foundations of the law enforcement in this town.

Now it's time to promote someone, and it shows that Johnny has been here a short time, and his arrests are up, his tickets are up, and he is the cool guy that the mayor remembers, so he gets it. Now Sergeant Johnny is in charge of the officers who have been there making things good for the citizens, and it's time to make budgetary changes. Well, Johnny needs money to buy faster cars, equipment to kick in doors, and bigger guns because that is the cool stuff he needs to do his heavy-handed, strong-arm police work he is used to doing that the administration and mayor see as successful. But what they are not seeing is the slow and steady crumbling of the trust in the local law enforcement.

People are losing their trust in law enforcement. They still know that faithful old officer has always been there, but his hands are tied because Sergeant Johnny is in control, and he is hiring all his friends who are getting promoted based on association and not customer satisfaction.

So this carries on for a while, and now Lieutenant Johnny is still working in his heavy-handed manner, and his arrests and going up, and now he has a SWAT team because he read that police shootings are up and trust of the police department is way down across the nation, and we have to prepare for that.

But 7 percent of the population commit all the crimes, so we MUST prepare for this coming onslaught of violence that is undoubtedly coming our way. We need more expensive bulletproof vests and Kevlar helmets because there was a bombing in New York City last week. The sky is falling. The sky is falling.

Officer Faithful asks for $100 to hold a community cookout to celebrate the coming of summer and hope to have a safe and happy summer break from school.

Lieutenant Johnny says, "Are you crazy? You're going to gather all these people up in one area and feed them? You will create a riot situation. Who is going to pay the overtime to have officers work this event? I need a plan of action to deploy the SWAT team before we even think about doing this. This is going to be far too expensive. There is no way we can possibly afford to take money away from the SWAT team training budget to have this pubic gathering. What was it for again? No, no way we can do this."

Police Administrator Johnny sees the one-time true statistic that 7 percent of the population commits all the crime as a call to action.

Police Officer Faithful sees the same statistic that 93 percent of the population don't commit crime and should be celebrated as a different call to action.

So here we are today. The need for jobs created a vacuum of overeducated people falling into public safety jobs making far less money than they thought they were worth and due to the piles of certificates and degrees that they came into the jobs with, they were promoted quickly into the positions of authority over the people who were probably meant for the jobs, who had a knack for the job, and who could reduce crime without much effort at all, and they overanalyzed their way into a deterioration of the foundations of law enforcement in America.

The same people who spent years in a classroom and had lost touch with the communities were now in a position to tell the beat cops how to connect with the communities and had no idea how to do it but had plenty of books to tell them that when a law is violated, you write a ticket.

It was always an interesting conversation for me to have with some of these people and have them explain their personal feelings on the letter of the law versus the spirit of the law. That is a dead giveaway on whether they can connect or truly get involved with the community.

You cannot throw a book at a problem and think it is going to fix it. Every community is different and unique but is wonderful and worthy of celebrating in its own right. If you're not spending time in your communities every day as a law enforcement officer you are drawing a check, you are not making a difference.

I fought to have my fellow officers spend time in the communities, and as young officers, they would do so and enjoy their time and get to know the community and see how they could make a difference just to have people higher in rank than me tell them that they were wasting their time.

I equate the current mindset of law enforcement to the difference between socialism and capitalism. We are living currently under a system of legal socialism instead of community capitalism.

It sounds extreme to put it that way, but you cannot attempt to rule any city or county with an iron fist of law enforcement.

You cannot have the mindset that you know better than the people you serve. In most instances, officers do not live in the communities they serve and oftentimes are not from the communities that they now work for, so in the eyes of the community, who are you to tell me what is good for me.

In our case, with Chief John Keohane, he didn't even live in the town where he was the chief of police, so why should the citizens think that its law enforcement has any feeling of concern for their well-being. There is a saying that holds true every time I say it or think it, "They don't care what you know until they know that you care." You can have all the knowledge in the world with the best of intentions, and it will not be received by the people that need it the most if you do not present it in a way that appears to be sincere.

I have told officers of all ranks that for years, and I have gotten responses from "okay", "well", "I understand that" to "then fuck 'em." If they don't want help, then move on and find someone who does want help. Unfortunately, the latter is more often the case than the previous.

Many people have argued that it is really not that important to have a chief of police that lives in town as long as he does a good job.

Here's a quote from a news article in the *New York Times*:

> And so much of the criticism of the police that has roiled the country over the past couple of years has centered on whether officers know the communities they patrol and understand the culture of the people who live in them.
>
> A version of this article appears in print on Aug. 19, 2016, on Page A10 of the New York edition with the headline: "In Milwaukee, Worries over Eliminating Rule That Police Must Live in City."

Across the United States, this question continues to arise. We are asking people to make the ultimate sacrifice every day and to make split-second decisions when they are not being given the right facilities and using their right faculties when taking on that ultimate responsibility.

Let me explain what I mean by that last statement.

 As police officers, we are constantly asking to be provided with all the most important new and improved gadgets to hang on our utility belt. We go to work every day and want to do the best job that we possibly can, and we are facing challenges to a certain degree, but we can only do so much with the hand that we are given. With the tools we are given, I call that the facilities we are provided. What we do with those facilities and how we utilize them are what I refer to as our faculties. The knowledge to handle our equipment the best way possible and to care for our equipment makes us efficient and care enough to do the best job possible.

One of the most important faculties that we can possibly have is the desire to do a good job. As in any job, the day-to-day desire to be the best at what we do is the driving force in one's ability to strive to be the greatest in the world. Everyone has at one time or another worked with someone who has come to work just to collect a paycheck, and they do just enough to get by. Their every thought was on what was going to happen after work or something that was going on somewhere else. In police work, you cannot afford to have people like that, but unfortunately, you do. And oftentimes, those are the people who live somewhere else, think they are doing a job that is beneath themselves, and should be doing their boss's job instead of the job they are in right now.

So when people discuss whether it is important for a chief of police to live in a community where they work, I say that it is not a choice. If your chief of police is not dedicated enough to your community to live in it and to be concerned with what is happening where he lives (your town), then he is working for the paycheck only. Police chiefs usually work for the retirement bump in pay and for the title to retire on. It is rare in today's climate to find a chief of police that is in it for the long haul. That is why I truly believe that you will not see many chiefs of police that will hold a tenure longer than that of five years anymore, or at least it will become more and more infrequent.

So I have always been one to feel like there cannot be a complaint without at least a thought of a way to fix it, and this is no different. Fixing law enforcement in American is going to take a systematic change, a commission like we saw in the thirties and the sixties and a change in the thought processes, which is going to hurt a lot of people.

But it is not going to hurt the people who matter. It is going to hurt the people who thought they were the superheroes or the wannabe Dick Tracy (1931), Pow Wow Smith (1949), and Sherlock Holmes (1887).

There must be a systematic change in the way we fund police departments. We cannot continue to fund police departments based on the number of crimes they enforce. That is a dollar-for-arrest basis. We are basically treating our police officers like strippers on a pole and telling them to go and shake your ass for dollars, and when they don't shake it well enough for Daddy, they are relegated to a job that no one wants or they are pushed aside or removed from the department for someone who is going to come in and put up the numbers or make the dollars that are required to advance the department the way that is needed in order to get the sky-is-falling equipment to keep Chief Johnny B. Goode happy.

My understanding of most local laws is that police departments cannot directly benefit from funds that are brought in from sales of confiscated property. But what is the real difference in sending officers out to specifically search for people violating traffic laws randomly. I worked as a traffic officer in Petersburg, Virginia, for a year, and I wrote more tickets than I can possibly recall. But as that year came to a close and I requested to move on to a different assignment, something became clear to me. Unless I was addressing a specific complaint about a specific problem in a specific area at a specific time at a specific, specific, specific, specific, I was just literally picking the pockets of people that were not benefiting from my service at all.

We as law enforcement officers have a job to do, and that is to help, fix, correct, or rescue. Randomly writing tickets doesn't achieve any of that other than to maybe address those issues for the budget of the department. But we are supposed to do those things for the citizens.

Here is a perfect example of what I mean. I was assigned to traffic in Petersburg, and I worked the midnight shift. I would sit in the area of West Washington Street near what is now the Governors

School in a 25 mph zone. It had been a 25 mph zone since the school was originally a school and was now abandoned, but the speed limit was never changed.

I was sitting there this particular morning, and a car came through at around 43 mph in a 25 mph zone. I pulled the car over, and the gentleman was upset that the speed limit was 25, but he knew it was 25, and he was speeding, so he got a ticket. Typical stop. Nothing out of the ordinary. On my way. The very next morning, I am working and I am sitting in the exact same spot at the exact same time at the exact same everything, and you guessed it. The same guy in the same car going around the same speed. I pulled him over. He was not happy at all, but we had a heated discussion about how stupid it was for the speed limit to be 25 mph, and he went on his way with another ticket.

So I am working the very next day in the exact same spot at the exact same time, and you guessed it. The same gentleman came through doing the same speed or within a couple miles an hour. This time, I said to him, "I don't need your driver's license. I believe I have memorized your information." He didn't have a whole lot to say this time, and after he signed his third ticket in three days, I said, "See you tomorrow."

His response was priceless. He said, "Hell no you won't. I'm going a different way from now on."

The bottom line is that if you are going to make a difference or a change in the way a certain traffic pattern works or the way a person drives, it is going to take something drastic. Driving is a habit, which is why they refer to them as your driving habits. My job as a traffic officer was to positively affect traffic patterns in the City of Petersburg, and there was speeding and reckless driving in that area. Being in the area routinely and writing tickets let people see that the police were taking a proactive approach to dealing with the issues.

This person obviously had more on his mind than fixing his driving issues and getting one ticket, or even two tickets was not enough to change his driving habits. So randomly taking money out of his wallet would have done nothing but created negative feelings toward the police and most likely, due to anger, created a worse driver than before.

So with all that being said, we make it a point to be clear about saying that we cannot directly benefit from the sale of confiscated property, but how much money does that really bring in? The good stuff is kept by the local departments anyway. It is not sold.

We write tickets and make arrests, and based on the number of those things reported to the state and federal government, we are provided funding to run our departments. More tickets and arrests mean more money for guns, cars, and cops.

But wait a minute, isn't one of the core principles of a police officer to protect and prevent crime? If that is the case, then wouldn't we be working ourselves out of a job if we are really good at what we do?

So with that theory in mind, we can determine which law enforcement administrations are the absolute worst in the country by judging which ones draw the most money from the state and federal government. Right? Because if you knew what you were doing, you wouldn't need so much money.

The job that my partner and I did in the public housing area of Hopewell, Virginia, created a 74 percent drop in crime, and we worked ourselves out of a job. The grant ended because the need was no longer there. Other officers were mad because "they don't do shit in housing" was what we used to hear all the time.

And they were right. But I took the job in the beginning because no one wanted it because it was going to be too much work, remember?

Black Lives Matter

I never had a problem with the Black Lives Matter movement, and I truly believe that most police officers don't either. They just don't want to speak against the vocal few who do.

I think that the movement in its core means that all lives matter and that includes Black lives, and to speak against Black lives is like saying that you don't think Black lives matter. I have Black family members, I am an elder in a predominantly Black church, and I was raised to see all people as equal and treat them the same until they choose to treat you differently, and then they get what they earn regardless of race.

To me, the movement was human lives matter and that includes Black lives, so I never had a problem with the core beliefs of what I know them to be. I have been a member of the NAACP, and even though I cannot say that I have agreed with everything they ever did, I cannot say that I have agreed with everything any group has ever done. I do, however, agree with any group that stands for the advancement of their race through self-education and justice for people who cannot stand up for themselves.

I am a Mason, which is in most people's minds contrary to being a member of the NAACP and believing in the Black Lives Movement. But at its core, the Masons, at least in Virginia, represent being the best man possible, and we acknowledge all Masons to include the Black Masons, as people like to refer to them. We are all brothers in the craft, and I have yet to be disrespected by a true Mason. The only people who I have ever run into that have ever had a problem with Masonry are people who are not Masons and for one reason or another will not be Masons or cannot be Masons.

There are many Masons in police work of all races and religions, and I have never seen that become an issue in police work, so if anything, that has been a uniting force in law enforcement.

Community policing has been by passion and in my blood from the time I was a small child. I can remember watching the few police officers that we had in the small town I grew up in just outside of Philadelphia. I went to school with his children, and I remember that he was a grossly, morbidly obese man, but he was respected by the whole town. That was curious to me. Mr. Danks was obviously great at what he did because he was respected. I remember his son Ernie from school, and his family seemed to be really happy. But it  was curious to me that he was so large. I wanted to be a police officer, but to me, you had to be able to do the job better than someone that large. How could he run or fight or jump?

What I didn't know at the time was that Mr. Danks didn't have to do all those things because of the type of guy that he was.

Now I don't really know that Mr. Danks was a great cop. I just know that we didn't seem to have much crime, and he was one of the few cops we had, so he must have been a great cop. He was to me, so that's all that mattered. I was young, and for all I know, Mr. Danks might not have really been that big. But in my juvenile mind and memory, he was a large man. Larger than life.

I have used Mr. Danks as an example many times in my life, and I have used his memory in my mind for many years that he is exactly what I do and don't want to be as a police officer. I want to have his level of respect, but I don't want to look like him and obviously lack the physical ability to do the job if needed. But where is the balance in all that?

How, as a law enforcement administrator, do you balance budgetary needs with our moral obligation to serve the public? We serve the public with the funds that are paid to us via the public we arrest and ticket. It just doesn't make a great deal of sense.

So how do you determine what money to give to what localities? Do you base it on population? Higher populations get higher amounts of money? That would be fairer than the way that they do it now. Under the pay for the crime statistics method they employ right now you are basically telling local police chiefs we want you to show progress but not too much progress.

How do you get credit for crimes that didn't happen? How do you prove crime prevention?

Let's look at corporate America. How do they rate their effectiveness in doing business?

CENTRAL
CHRISTIAN
COLLEGE
OF KANSAS
ONLINE

5 Strategies to Improve Organizational Effectiveness
CCCK Online
August 18, 2016

1. Make Use of Human Resources
2. Focus on Education and Growth
3. Keep the Customers in Mind
4. Work on Quality Services or Products
5. Use Technology

8 Ways to Empower Your Employees to Be More Productive
www.americanexpress.com

1. Get Out of the Kitchen
   Let people do their jobs without interfering.
2. Fling the Door Wide Open on Information
   Not sharing information is the most disempowering thing you can do.
3. Establish Quality Circles
   Quality circles are an empowering alternative to keeping employees boxed within the narrow confines of their compartmentalized functions.
4. Enrich Jobs
   Give people more authority within their functional areas.

5. Let Employees Make Decisions

Nothing kicks employees' personal power into high gear more than having a voice in the decision-making process.

6. Update Your Technology Policies

Don't restrict your employees from using their own social tools at work.

7. Allow Some Corporate Breathing Space

Working in a stifling environment snuffs the life out of enthusiasm and initiative.

8. Lower Employee Stress

If people are stressed, their focus will be more on minimizing their stress by paying attention to what keeps them safe.

Corporate America has always been able of keeping their profits up over time, and if you learn from the larger companies that have been around for years, you will be ahead of the game.

So how do we translate the corporate mindset into community policing? Let's use the American Express example above and make it a community policing example.

1. Get Out of the Patrol Car

Let people do their jobs without interfering.

2. Fling the Investigative Door Wide Open on Information

Not sharing information is the most disempowering thing you can do.

3. Establish Quality Community Circles

Quality community circles are an empowering alternative to keeping employees boxed within the narrow confines of their compartmentalized functions.

4. Enrich Job Functions

Give people more adaptability within their job function areas.

5. Let Officers Make Decisions

Nothing kicks officers' personal motivation into high gear more than having a voice in the decision-making process.

6. Update and Expand Your Technology Policies

    Don't restrict your employees from using their own social tools at work, expand them as much as possible, and include your young officers in this. They know what works.

7. Allow Some Administrative Breathing Space

    Working in a stifling environment snuffs the life out of enthusiasm and initiative. Include an administrator with the daily operations but only as oversight and take part as a worker, not a decision maker.

8. Lower Officer Stress

    If officers are stressed, their focus will be more on minimizing their stress by paying attention to what keeps them safe. Recognize the good and minimize the bad.

Have our agencies always been able to do these things? Of course, they have, but they most often never do. Ask your veteran officers if these things are being done, and if your agency is floundering, I would bet you that they aren't happening.

So why does it seem that law enforcement treats African Americans and those of races other than Whites worse than any others?

I attribute that to several factors. First, the news doesn't care if a White officer fights with a White criminal. I don't know the statistics on it, but I know that it occurs. Second, there is very little fear of it getting out of hand and becoming front-page news since the news doesn't care. Throughout history, there is not a long history of White-on-White crime that has built up fear in the hearts of White men across the country to fear the police. There are no movies, songs, raps, or plays depicting White-on-White crime, police beating White men, or any other sensationalized White victims of police brutality. As a Caucasian male in America, I was raised to respect the police regardless of their race or sex.

On the contrary, many Asians and Hispanics come from cultures that, in their homelands, dealt with extremely crooked and brutal law enforcement agencies that supplemented their incomes off the backs of the blood, sweat, and tears of the very people that we are now dealing with and are either here legally or illegally seeking the American dream.

For those here illegally, they fear being deported back to those countries that they risked their lives to leave and may face retribution for running away from. Oftentimes, the money they make under the table here in the United States is enough to support their entire families back in Central America or Mexico. So they have much more to lose by dealing with the police than we may understand.

And African Americans, in many cases, were raised watching *Boys in the Hood, Colors, New Jersey Drive,* and the whole gambit of Spike Lee movies that show the way many African Americans have been treated in America. Not to mention, we look at history class and learn from the riots and clashes with police that have occurred in this country over the last one hundred years, but we expect everyone to "just do as you are told, and everything will be okay."

Let's look at a few examples of how everything was okay.

- Robert Gisevius, Kenneth Bowen, and Anthony Villavaso
  These three were members of the New Orleans Police Department during Hurricane Katrina. They were charged with first-degree murder for killing seventeen-year-old James Brissette, who was innocent and unarmed during Hurricane Katrina on the Danzinger Bridge. Brisette was simply looking for shelter from the hurricane, and the cops pounced on him.
- Jon Burge
  Jon Burge is a former Chicago Police Department detective who oversaw the torture of hundreds of Black men, resulting in false confessions between 1972 and 1991.
  Burge would burn suspects with radiators and cigarettes, and electrocute their testicles.
  Although Burge was protected by the statute of limitations for his crimes, he was convicted for lying about the torture in January of this year.

- Joseph Miedzianowski

  Joseph Miedzianowski was a Chicago police officer labeled as the most corrupt cop. Miedzianowski served as both police officer and drug kingpin, using his knowledge of the streets and gangs to shake down drug dealers.

  For most of his twenty-two-year career, Miedzianowski would run the Chicago Gangs Unit, while running his own drug gang at the same time. Miedzianowski would be convicted of ten counts, including drug conspiracy and racketeering in 2001.

While these all seem like extreme cases, there are things like this happening all over the United States every day. In Hopewell, there were things occurring that just never hit the news, but the public new about it. The administration took care of it, and usually, the people went away, and in some cases, the officers stayed and ended up being promoted on to captain.

One case, we will call him John, was when an officer who was in with the drug boys would tip them off every time we were going to be in a certain part of town and anytime we were going to be doing a search warrant, and in the end, they bought him a car and put an extension on his house  when his wife gave birth to their youngest child. The drug boys were untouchable for so long because they always knew we were coming. But all it took was one arrest by the feds in a different jurisdiction, and they gave him up. Did he get arrested? Nope. He was stripped of his time as a police officer toward retirement, told he could never work as a police officer again, and shown the door.

Detective M, who went on to be Sergeant M, was not at all the brightest tool in the shed. He worked the drug task force, midnight patrol, and lots of

other assignments that he never really seemed to excel at. But the administration kept him around because he was comfortably numb, as I like to put it. Not smart enough to argue, just dumb enough to do whatever he was told and without question. He loved the midnight shift, and as I was told, he used to love to shake down the drug boys, would take their drug money, and sometimes take the drugs too. But he never arrested them. Who were they going to complain to? Nice way to supplement his income. If they complained too much, he would arrest them or call one of us over to help him and let us find the drugs and make the arrest.

Detective R was great with the kids and would go out of his way to always be there for the kids and that was a fact. But rumor had it that he was always in the projects with the ladies when he was off duty. He worked on some of the task forces too. He had a lot of power but got a monkey on his back with alcohol. He got stopped drinking and driving. Arrested? Nope. Go home. Stopped again the same night, still drinking. Arrested? Nope. Go home. Stopped again. Crash! Arrested? Eventually. He could have killed someone, but he is back working in law enforcement now. Is that someone to trust?

And the whopper, Officer Mark. He used to be obese. Now he is skinny and a cop. He was the king of the DUI stop on women. He made lots of arrests and even more stops without arrests. Officers noticed that things were shady. Administration loved lots of arrests. Then the story broke. "You can do me a favor or I can arrest you." Is this the cop you trust?

Sergeant P was so in with the administration that he was cycling buddies with the chief. He could do no wrong. Drinking with his subordinates or fighting in the streets, all was forgiven and be damned if anyone should even mention that there was anything wrong with that. He got involved in a DUI hit-and-run and got arrested, and did the administration seek justice for the citizen? No! We think he can be saved. He just made a mistake. They tried to keep it under wraps, and if he got jail time, they wanted it to be with the local sheriff on weekends. He could still work as a police officer with a restricted driver's license to and from work, while at work, etc. Keep him on the books getting paid while the court case is being addressed, working in animal control so his family doesn't have to suffer. Where is the justice for the person who was feloniously mistreated? And it almost worked out for him until the news got a hold of it. But who told them? Apparently, two or three of his own coworkers just couldn't stand to see him get over again and let the news know that this was going on. But this was a leader among the guys we are supposed to trust.

But remember these are the people that we are just expecting the public to just trust. And this is just one small town, 10.5 square miles in the middle of the East Coast of the United States. A blue-collar town that anyone should be proud to be from. Is this happening in all small towns across America?

Is it time for a new Federal Commission to investigate the crumbling of American law enforcement? The system we have is designed to compensate those agencies with high numbers when it comes to activity. So how do you compensate those agencies that have accomplished their goals of curtailing crime? When do we learn to reward for our accomplishments instead of feeding bad behavior?

Racial Profiling, Does It Exist?

1. Using race or ethnicity as grounds for suspecting someone of having committed an offense
2. Carrying out research or study into (a subject, typically one in a scientific or academic field) so as to discover facts or information

Here are two definitions that come into play in *law enforcement*. One is absolutely and totally illegal and could make you end up in prison, and the other will make you without a doubt one of the best cops ever to live. I think that you will see that although it is very easy to see the difference between the two, they are dangerously similar and that is the basis for many officers to be disgruntled.

I recall testifying one time when I was young and new to police work in Petersburg when I had my attention drawn to a small Honda two-door vehicle driving up and down Halifax Street at 3:00 a.m. because there were two young White males driving the car. After a few minutes of following the vehicle, I observed a traffic violation and pulled the car over, and in plain sight, I saw a bag of what I believed to be marijuana on the center console of the vehicle. I took the driver into custody for the suspected marijuana and issued him a summons.

Well, that was how it eventually went. How I testified in court was "I stopped the car because they were White, Your Honor." I think Judge Beck just about choked, heard the case, and immediately called me back to his chambers to instruct me on correct process for testimony. I had all what I needed for the case, but I didn't testify correctly.

In the two instances above, one can be done alone, the other cannot. The second one listed is the definition of an investigation. The first one listed is obviously the definition of racial profiling. Number 1 can be used as a portion of number 2, but number 1 can never be used alone.

If you are given information as a portion of an investigation that a certain race of person was involved, then you obviously can use that portion of a profile as a part of your investigation. But you cannot start your investigation looking at only one race of people with no other information.

Many people used to make the case that terrorists are easy to pick out. We know the nationality or at least the general region of the world where they will come from. We know generally how they will strike, etc.; then we had Timothy McVeigh of Oklahoma City bombing fame and the DC Sniper, and our ideas that perhaps racial profiling was useful went right out the window.

Good Guys

What is the psychology behind the police uniform, police cars, and police behavior?

We used to be taught to do certain things, not do certain things, and drive a certain vehicle. But that, to me, was rooted in the American past. Let's start with the car. Now this is my opinion or at least my understanding of how or why things used to be the way they were and maybe how they should be back to the way they are.

Police cars

Description: two toned, essentially easy to identify, and lacking any threat

Police officer

Description: hat and tie, essentially easy to identify, and lacking any threat

There are certain things that we teach our children to look for when they are in trouble or in need of help. That is why the police

125

cars were two toned and why the police officers wore hats, wore coats, and had ties. They looked respectable and easily identifiable. Now let's look at how things may have changed over the last few years.

Police cars

Description: dark in color, threatening in nature

Police officers

Description: often no hat or tie, glasses, threatening manner, unfriendly

As a part of Crisis Intervention Training that I was an instructor for, we taught officers to give people their names when speaking to them. Officers would lose their minds. "I am not telling anyone my name" or "They don't need to know my name".

We would have to spend a great deal of time going over with them the unfortunate fact that the public happens to know everything about them whether they like it or not. So if we have officers who aren't willing to give the public their name, how can we possibly get the police officers to feel a connection with the public that they work for?

Here is a quick news flash to all law enforcement across America and the world. Unless you are a private pay security force, your bosses are all the citizens of the world who happen to pay taxes, and quite honestly, if they want to know your name, they have the right to know that. So much so that many police departments have started moving toward using name tags that have the officer's first name on them.

We cannot continue to try and make people believe that we really care about them while refusing to give them our first names. They know what your name is, where you live, what you drive, whether you are married, and what your dog's names are. You might as well act like you care.

So Why Is This Happening Nationwide?

Let's take a look at some Regional Police Academy curriculums and see just how important community engagement/community policing really is. Well, for that sake, let's see just how important the job of PREVENTING CRIME is to our training academies. After all, the job of a law enforcement officer should be to stop crime before it happens too, right?

First stop, and only because it was the first agency to come up on an internet search.

REGIONAL POLICE ACADEMY OF KANSAS CITY—TRAINING CURRICULUM			
Name	Code#	Hours	Lecture
Crime Prevention	802	4	4

GEORGIA PEACE OFFICER STANDARDS OF TRAINING	
OFFICER AND THE PUBLIC	2 HOURS
COMMUNITY POLICING & CRIME PREVENTION	4 HOURS

CALIFORNIA COMMISSION ON PEACE OFFICER
STANDARDS AND TRAINING

TRAINING AND TESTING
SPECIFICATIONS FOR LEARNING DOMAIN #13 18 HOURS
POLICING IN THE COMMUNITY

MISSISSIPPI PEACE OFFICER
STANDARDS & TRAINING

FULL-TIME AND PART-TIME LAW ENFORCEMENT OFFICER
HAVE NO IDENTIFIED COURSES RELATED TO COMMUNITY POLICING
AND CRIME PREVENTION IN THEIR STANDARDS AND TRAINING

Connecticut Police Officer Standards and Training

Crime Prevention	2 hours
Police and the Public	2 hours

Arizona Administrative Code

Functional Area VI—Community and Police Relations
    I. Cultural awareness
    II. Victimology
    III. Interpersonal communications
    IV. Crime prevention
    V. Police and the community
    NO SPECIFIC HOUR REQUIREMENTS ARE LISTED, JUST THAT THESE
ARE INCLUDED IN THE REQUIRED TOPICS FOR THE BASIC CERTIFICATION

STATE OF ALABAMA REQUIREMENTS

RULE 6500-4-.01 Education requirements
    HAVE NO IDENTIFIED COURSES RELATED TO COMMUNITY POLICING
AND CRIME PREVENTION IN THEIR STANDARDS AND TRAINING

There are many states that make it incredibly difficult to find the actual course descriptions that are the standards for the basic law enforcement recruit classes. I understand that because it SHOULD be a living, breathing document that is ever changing, but it should still list community and crime prevention somewhere in the standards, and as you see above, there are a few that don't even list crime prevention as a standard in their academies.

Wonder why we are losing the battle to crime? We aren't doing anything to beat it; we are just trying to figure it out after it happens. We are chasing our tails and thinking we are getting ahead.

So this is why I say that we need a systematic change in the way we go about policing in the United States. We have to change the way we are addressing crime. If you always chase the criminal instead of trying to change the mindset, you will never win.

I have been a part of the Big Brothers Big Sisters Program for four years now and out of around sixty police officers there were only two of us that took part in the program, and the other one besides me was one of the many officers I trained as a young officer who was amazing and is now a sergeant and doing big things. We are not instilling a community mindset in our police officers as they learn the basics and then wondering why they don't get it later.

You can't teach an old dog new tricks, so why are we trying to teach old cops techniques that they should have known from the beginning?

How many officers are assigned to community programs in your jurisdiction? Most jurisdictions have perhaps one or two trying to work with your community partners to establish programs that can benefit your department and the community.

Your communities see that you only put one person into the interest of the community, and it shows that you don't really care.

TO NEIGHBORHOOD WATCH OR NOT TO NEIGHBORHOOD WATCH? THAT IS THE QUESTION

So I was working as the community relations officer in the Hopewell Police Department, and I had the number 3 ranked officer in the whole city come to me and ask, "Do you really need to be going to these neighborhood watch meetings? I don't need to pay you overtime for these meetings."

Thinking he was joking, I started laughing and didn't answer. Realizing that he was still standing there and looking at me, I looked at him a few minutes later and realized he was waiting for an answer. I said, "Captain T, you're serious? These citizens are taking time out of their lives to come to a meeting and help us to help them keep crime down in their neighborhoods. The least we can do is to go to the meeting and hear what they feel like the problems are in the neighborhoods."

Captain T agreed and just wanted me to make sure I cleared up as soon as possible since the meetings were on my time and I was being paid overtime.

This is the mindset of most police administrations. I don't think they understand the true value and advantage of a strong neighborhood watch program. We in law enforcement talk about how we need the public to share information with us all the time and how we want to build bridges to better communication, but we aren't willing to have those bridges in place unless we need the information in a tragedy. We aren't willing to do the work when the need isn't there. We aren't willing to do the work on a day-to-day basis when the public needs us to talk to their kids who are acting up and won't listen because of course "it's not our job to raise your kids" or "we have more important things to do."

No, we don't. Our jobs are to get in touch with the public and stay in touch with the public, and if that means taking the calls to speak to the kids who aren't listening to their parents, then that's what we do because we don't have anything more important to do. That is how we keep from becoming detached from the public we serve. But that is the part of police work that I spoke about when I said that the Johnny B. Goodes don't want to do it. Officer Dependable has always done it and was there to do it, and everyone knew they could count on them to do it.

It's the boring and mundane parts of police work that the public needs us to do that makes us dependable and makes us the people who they can count on and makes us the people who they can turn to when they need us.

Do you ever wonder why police officers don't ride two to a car anymore? I asked that once, and I was told that it caused too many fights. But how does that make sense? The background behind that was that if a police officer responded to a disturbance, they would have to try and resolve the disturbance while waiting for their backup, and hopefully, it would be resolved before their backup got there. So officers had to rely on their ability to talk, or at least they had to be in shape and have a great ability to fight.

How about the implementation of cameras? Good thing or bad thing? I originally thought that they would be a good thing, but I got an education from Judge Beck in Petersburg Traffic Court who refused to look at the VHS tapes of traffic stops, and I loved his explanation for it.

I would tell him that I had a video of a certain traffic stop or DUI, and he would tell me over and over that he was not interested in seeing the tapes. I finally asked him in his chambers once that he would not ask to see the tapes unless he was forced to do so in the courtroom because once he started looking at the tapes, it would represent a shift in his belief in what I testified to as an officer of the law. By his watching the tapes, he was essentially saying to me, "I don't believe what you are testifying to, so I am going to watch the tape for myself and see what really happened."

Once I really let that soak in, it had a huge impact on me for the remainder of my career. I found that I despised cameras of any kind after that, except maybe still cameras in order to show to judges and juries evidence. But video cameras were always detrimental to me. I would find that they would be used by the police department numerous times in the future in order to discipline officers who they wanted to keep under their thumb, not everyone, just their select few.

Body cameras have been introduced to law enforcement and the courts, which have now created the shadow of doubt and allowed for everyone to question everything they saw. If it's not on camera, then you must be a liar. If even a minute detail is different than you stated, then you must be a liar, regardless of the level of stress. Even if you give a dead-on description of the events that transpired, if I misinterpreted what you said, then you must be a liar. Body cameras are subject to interpretation by the person watching and listening, and therefore, they are like NFL instant replays. If you aren't the home team, then you are going to be mad if you don't get the call.

I find it extremely interesting that body cameras are so extremely important while at work in law enforcement but are forbidden when you are called to speak to your supervisor or the magistrate. Yes, a policy came out in Hopewell that basically said that we could not record either audio or visual any conversation between the officer and supervisor while at work. I find that amazingly curious since what they are supposedly doing as our supervisors and the leaders of law enforcement should at all times be legal and in the best interest of society.

I had a pen that I used to use at work often that had a camera in it and got amazingly good reception. Well, I used it one time during a discussion I was having with several of my bosses, but something happened, and it started to play back right in the middle of the conversation. Well, that was when the policy came out about not having recording devices when meeting with supervisors. The real funny part of that was that anytime I spoke with a supervisor after that, they would ask where my pen was.

So it gives new meaning to the saying that the pen is mightier than the sword. The body cameras were such a great idea, yet they were banned while speaking to a supervisor and at headquarters. Why? I wonder if the public is aware of this and how they would feel about it if they were to be asked.

So in my personal and professional opinion, I have always felt like anyone who identifies a problem without a solution is just a whiner. So what is the answer to the question? What is wrong with law enforcement in America. Where do we go?

There must be a systematic evaluation of where you have been, where you are, and most importantly, where the public believes you are. All this must be assessed before any forward movement can be made.

Just as in determining what the needs of the public are, determining what the needs of the individual department are is just as important. Determining what the needs of the department are can be a rather laborious and problematic process. Wading through the same hurdles that got many departments in shambles that they are in to begin with will undoubtedly be a problem for whomever is tasked with beginning this evaluation process.

So exactly what information needs to be gathered? There needs to be a complete evaluation of past efforts, community partner call to arms (per se), a complete community needs assessment, a department needs evaluation, and a unification of all the information, a sort of groundbreaking on the road to recovery if things have been bad, or a ribbon cutting into the future for agencies that things have not gotten bad.

Either way, it takes a realistic look at the past, present, and future of the community, and it takes a real partnership with the community and a realization that you cannot continue to police the community without the community being on your team. There should be community review boards for internal affairs complaints, community review boards for hiring and firing, and community police academies to keep the community as a part of your team. If you are not doing all these things, then you are not working with your community. You are trying to police the community instead of policing with the community.

The law enforcement officer who has it in his blood to do this job will welcome the public because that is the job at its core. That is who we live to serve. The cops who do this job for the paycheck or who got into this job because of who they know or because of the fast cars or heavy hands they thought they could have, like the guys they watched on TV, will fear the involvement of the public into the decision-making process. They will see the community presence as an intrusion into a job that they couldn't possibly understand.

For many of us, the hiring process for law enforcement required many steps, from a physical test, to a written test, to a psychological test, to a series of interviews. One of which involved some community partners.

The community partner interview that I did for the Petersburg Police Department included four to five civilians, one of which was a local preacher. That interview was probably the one that made me the most nervous because I was most anxious to please the public.

There was actually a government action that mandated change in many ways we are dealing with crime in the United States. It is called the Violent Crime Control and Law Enforcement Act of 1994. But has it done any good? Let's look this over and see what has been put in place, and then we can discuss whether it has made a difference.

TITLE I—PUBLIC SAFETY AND POLICING

Sec. 10001. Short title.
Sec. 10002. Purposes.
Sec. 10003. Community policing; "Cops on the Beat"

Right in the beginning, it starts off mentioning *community policing*.

TITLE II—PRISONS

The next few sections deal with a great number of topics relating to incarceration, truth in sentencing, and youthful offenders.

TITLE III—CRIME PREVENTION
Subtitle A.—Ounce of Prevention Council

Sec. 30101. Ounce of Prevention Council.
Sec. 30102. Ounce of prevention grant program.
Sec. 30103. Definition.
Sec. 30104. Authorization of appropriations.

Subtitle B.—Local Crime Prevention Block Grant Program

Sec. 30201. Payments to local governments.
Sec. 30202. Authorization of appropriations.
Sec. 30203. Qualification for payment.
Sec. 30204. Allocation and distribution of funds.
Sec. 30205. Utilization of private sector.
Sec. 30206. Public participation.
Sec. 30207. Administrative provisions.
Sec. 30208. Definitions.

One Hundred Third Congress of the United States of America
AT THE SECOND SESSION
Begun and held at the City of Washington on Tuesday, the twenty-fifth day of January, one thousand nine hundred and ninety-four.
An Act to control and prevent crime.

The Violent Crime Control and Law Enforcement Act of 1994 spells out all the steps required to either start or continue to build a strong community. It speaks of delegating moneys to go to youth programs and to unemployment.

It even stated very clearly about developing other programs that contribute to the community.

So now we have found three examples of times in the history of our country where the government of the United States of America has taken the time, money, and effort to enact something that investigated and/or spelled out the problems with our society as it relates to crime and what our country needs to do as it moves forward.

The Wickersham Commission in the 1920s, the *Kerner Report* in the 1960s, and now the Violent Crime Control and Law Enforcement Act of 1994. So here we are approaching the next evolution of our society where we are going to require that our government assign a committee to tell us again how to be law enforcement officers, just to have our existing police administrations ignore them again.

Believe me, I am not implying that I know all the existing law enforcement administrations and know that they will all ignore the recommendations of our government. What I am implying is that the previous three government actions that told us exactly what needed to be done were completely ignored. The most recent government action was in 1994, so if any of our administrations had power in 1994, then perhaps they may not be the most reliable to lead us into the next generation of law enforcement leadership.

I believe that we have identified the problem time and time again over nearly one hundred years of history in this country. What we have not done is identify the method by which we implement those changes. The reason that those changes have not been successfully implemented is because it requires you to tell the Chief Johnny B. Goodes in power to forget what they know and listen to the Officer John Q. Public, who had always known what to do.

It requires you to listen to the average John Q. Public officer who knows the public and has the trust of the public to implement the programs that they have probably been campaigning for all along. It will require the police administrations to swallow their pride and admit that perhaps their bust-that-ass-and-ask-questions-later attitude wasn't the right thing to do after all.

And most importantly, it requires the law enforcement administrations to humble themselves and reach out to the public and approach their communities and learn what a community partner is and, in some cases, tuck their tails and ask for help in making community connections to rebuild the bridges that were burned so long ago.

I would love to see just one agency of any size take any one of the previous reports and implement it. Don't necessarily tell anyone what they are doing. Wait until they have had a chance to get some feedback from the public, but use it as a public experiment. I would bet you that there would be more successes than failures, even if you were to utilize the *Wickersham Report* from the 1930s.

So I will end with what I believe is the best example of a community police officer that I know of, Officer Tommy Norman of North Little Rock, Arkansas. Most people know who Tommy Norman is. But let's see what has occurred to Mr. Norman after all the great things he has done to bridge the gap between the races in Little Rock, Arkansas, and how he has made such an impact on the lives of the youth, the homeless, the young, and old. Here is an article to show how his police administration rewarded his actions.

North Little Rock Police Officer Tommy Norman, Who Is
Known for the Amazing Interactions with the Community
He Polices, Posted a Video on Wednesday Saying that
He Can Longer Post Such Videos While On-Duty.
Michael Buckner, *KTHV*, June 28, 2017

NORTH LITTLE ROCK, Ark. (KTHV)—
North Little Rock police officer Tommy Norman,
who is known for the amazing interactions with
the community he polices, posted a video on
Wednesday saying that he can longer post such
videos while on-duty. In a video, Norman said
he was informed by superiors within the police
department that he cannot post photos or videos on his social media pages while wearing his
badge.

"There's a policy in effect at the police department that prohibits you from posting on-duty
that is now going to be enforced," he said.

Norman said he has to respect the decision
despite being unhappy with it.

Recently, Norman received an outpouring of support after helping a pregnant homeless woman
and her baby while on-duty.

He said he had to help the domestic abuse sur-
vivor and was amazed by the response of people
willing to "make a difference to change this family's life."

"Don't give up on me, I was born to do this,"
Norman said, before ending the video.

In response, the North Little Rock Police Department said they did not tell Norman that he couldn't post on social media.

The department said they made Norman aware of a policy and any posts had to be approved through the Media Relations Unit.

"The department greatly supports the work that Officer Norman has done and will continue to do in our community," the police department said in a statement.

To see what is right, and not to do it, is
want of courage or of principle.

—Confucius

Mark Twain Can Explain It All Away

I have always been a great admirer of Mark Twain. His down-to-earth wit and his "punch 'em in the gut" humor always appealed to me. Here are a few quotes that fit this circumstance perfectly.

First, to explain a few reasons why we are in the mess we are in:

The lack of money is the root of all evil.

Get your facts first, then you can distort them as you please.

Don't go around saying the world owes you a living. The world owes you nothing. It was here first.

And next to explain what we do about it:

> If you tell the truth, you don't have to remember anything.

> The secret of getting ahead is getting started.

> Kindness is the language which the deaf can hear and the blind can see.

And maybe a few just to make you think:

> Whenever you find yourself on the side of the majority, it is time to pause and reflect.

> Keep away from people who try to belittle your ambitions. Small people always do that, but the really great make you feel that you, too, can become great.

> I have never let my schooling interfere with my education.

A FEW THINGS TO CONSIDER
IN A BROKEN WORLD

I have stated over and over that crime is money, and the higher the crime, the more money you will get to fight that crime, and in essence, you will not want to actually win the fight because then you will lose the money.

But it actually goes further than that. The system we have to fight crime and dole out justice is hinged upon money and the criminals that cause us to need the system in the first place.

I have always known that as we write less and less traffic tickets, it affects the courts. Fewer court cases cause the money being given to the courts to drop, but I wasn't sure exactly how that works, so I decided to look into it to see if I could find anything concrete.

What I found was quite interesting.

Quoting the National Center for State Courts, Virginia:

Virginia
State/Local Funding
• The Virginia Judiciary is funded primarily by the state
• The state pays for the Appellate Courts and the Administrative Office of the Courts, for the salaries of trial court judges and trial court clerical staff and for trial court technology and operating expenses. Trial court judicial support staff and local courthouses and equipment are paid by local funding bodies.

Funding Principles for Judicial Administration
- The FY13 budget does not enable the courts to provide or enhance necessary technology to meet the demands of the public.
  Business Processes: The Virginia courts have implemented remote videoconferencing of incarcerated defendants and detained juveniles and remote videoconferencing of interpreters for persons with limited English proficiency.

The *Virginia courts are in a worse position* than in FY09 to provide access and timely justice, primarily due to improvements: inuchno/ogy. If the budget situation improves, they will fill existing judicial vacancies.

So by improving the technology and streamlining the judicial process, it has caused the courts to be in a "worse position" than they were in the past. This is a perfect example of how our system is NOT built to improve.

If officers are out in the community and making an impact on areas that are commonly monitored such as roadway safety, you SHOULD see an initial increase in traffic stops, summonses, written warnings, and verbal warnings. If these roadway safety efforts are focused and meaningful to the jurisdiction, they would address specific areas of concern that perhaps were based on previous year's statistical review of accidents, speeding, and violations.

Spending time in those areas would seemingly create a system of "fixing" the problems with the roadway safety issues and therefore create an eventual decrease in the number of traffic stops, summonses, written warnings, and verbal warnings. This being a focused approach to dealing with crime or safety, it would seem to result in an eventual positive end result for the community and the jurisdiction as a whole.

BUT—and there is always a but—allowing an officer to remain in one area long enough to actually complete a roadway safety project where the end result is a decrease in activity would result in a statistical "loss" or in the mind of most law enforcement administrations, a lack of productivity.

So in the end, the supposed attempt to address roadway safety is just an attempt to write some tickets long enough to slow things down and move on to the next "hot spot" and then let things heat back up again.

We have seen that the courts are not technologically advanced, or if they are, it creates an issue with them being in a "worse position" because they become more efficient and therefore less needy.

An issue came up years ago with the speed limit in Virginia being increased to 70 mph on the interstates. People loved it until they realized that reckless driving is still 80 mph and reckless driving is very expensive. That alone created a huge funding boom for the courts in Virginia.

Crime is money. If there are no speed limits in the United States over 70 mph, then why do we have cars that go over 70? Wouldn't the world be safer and more efficient if we couldn't go over 70 anyway? Just think, no car chases by the police that go 100 plus miles per hour, the fastest car chase would be 70 and the police could have cars that go faster so people could never get away. So why allow cars to go 130 mph out of the factory if it is illegal?

So the courts are not designed to be efficient, the laws and the police have a financial system that is dependent on keeping a high crime rate, and we don't adequately train our officers in community policing and crime prevention. But we are hopeful that our future will be filled with a reduction in crime and a less crowded courts system.

Why would be expect that to occur?

How many agencies are being rewarded for having a more efficient system in place? For having a more successful grant program and for most efficiently spending the money that they received for the grant?

How many grant administrators are being audited to ensure that they are evenly distributing the grant funds throughout the commonwealths and states rather than the ones that they live closest to or their friends are in?

Maybe there is an audit system in place, but it never seemed to create a fair and equitable distribution of funds for South Central

Virginia. But you can bet that Fairfax gets the millions every year because they are chock-full of crime, over and over and over and over.

It's time for a system that rewards successes and acknowledges those that are being innovative and we start policing ourselves instead of promoting a system of locker room banter among the boys who are going to cover each other's heavy-handedness until it gets caught on camera and everyone is talking about how they always knew he was a bad guy.

Police arrests are increasing at an alarming rate, and if we don't pay attention to it and stop it now, it is only going to increase even quicker. The *Washington Post* article cited below has an increase of almost 50 percent in five years from 2006–2011. So what are we doing to address it?

(For example, the study found that 22 percent of the officers arrested had been named as defendants in a federal civil rights lawsuit at some point in their careers, unrelated to their arrest case. The authors suggest that police agencies analyzing such suits "could potentially lead to new and improved mechanisms to identify and mitigate various forms of police misconduct.")

Here is a benchmark. Perhaps there needs to be some sort of review process for all officers that are named in federal civil rights lawsuits prior to being cleared to return to normal duty. This review should be from an outside source. We may find a way to at least catch 22 percent of the violators.

At a glance, from 2005 to 2011, there were a total of 6,724 police arrest cases.

1,238 cases

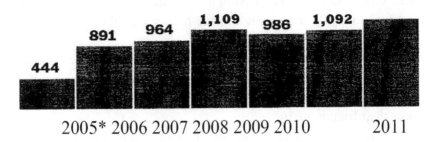

2005* 2006 2007 2008 2009 2010　　2011

58.5% arrested involve off duty officers

41.5% arrested on duty officers

94.5% involve male

*Note: The number of cases in 2005 is significantly lower than other years because the researchers were developing methodology.

An area breakdown

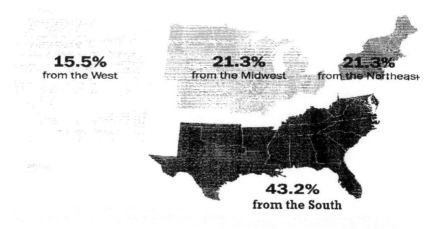

15.5% from the West

21.3% from the Midwest

21.3% from the Northeast

43.2% from the South

Source: "Police Integrity Lost: A Study of Law Enforcement Officers Arrested" by Philip Matthew Stinson Sr., John Liederbach, Steven P. Lab and Steven L. Brewer Jr. WEIYI CAI/THE WASHINGTON POST
True Crime
Study finds police officers arrested 1,100 times per year, or 3 per day, nationwide
By Tom Jackman
June 22, 2016

It even tells us where to begin the examination process to make the highest impact immediately.

I wonder why the incidents of police arrest are so much higher in the Southeastern United States. More than double the Northeast and Midwest and almost triple the West.

It's time to wake up and create a system that actually invites real change and rewards good behavior and success.

ANY IDEAS?

BWCs—body-worn cameras. Such a great idea but the problem is…

As stated in numerous articles and research papers plastered all over the internet, body-worn cameras are great, they are the devil, the "don't work when you need them to." They are everything and nothing.

So if that is the case, why is the federal government spending the millions of dollars that they are to continually fund body-worn camera grants?

Agencies like the ACLU and NAACP have brought articles and issues up with the government asking questions like "Where is the line that suggests the public's breach of privacy has been crossed?"

We were always told that we should film every interaction with the public, but as soon as we came to headquarters and had to meet with an administrator, for any reason we were not to be filming anything. Why?

So often the real dangerous crimes that really need the videotape are not caught on tape because under the stress of the call, the officer forgot to activate the camera. Or in my case, my camera was malfunctioning and after three days of notifying my supervisor, I got a new camera and written up anyway for not filming for three days. Yeah, figure that one out.

So let's take out the human element. Let's take out all question of privacy issues and let's stop putting this all on the officer's shoulders to have yet another thing that has to be done in the midst of a traumatic call for service.

Let's have the federal government continue to fund the body-worn camera programs as they have all along and let's have a lot more oversight of the money that is being spent. Let's get a government contract for the best price and offer the cameras to the police departments that want them and they will be funded as always. But the local law enforcement agencies will have steps to go through in order to get copies of the videos.

So we can ensure that the cameras are ALWAYS on.

Officer A comes to work, gets a BWC, and puts it on, and it is activated and running until he or she leaves to go home. The camera will send the video to the Cloud and it will be safely stored and the public's privacy is safe, and we know that all interaction with law enforcement is recorded. No "I forgot to turn it on" as an excuse, or reviewing the camera before figuring out the lie on the report. And the public will have the same processes to go through to obtain a copy of the BWC footage for court if they so request it.

Good for the police and good for the public. The government can ensure that they are getting the best bang for their buck when it comes to purchasing BWCs, and all footage of law enforcement activity is recorded and safely stored to ensure everyone's privacy is safe.

Let's take the question marks out of everyone's hands and put the ability to concentrate on the job back in the mind of the officer that is busting his/her butt out there to do an amazing job.

BWC footage should be available to everyone via subpoena or official request and cost for copies of footage can be paid to the company that is storing the information, if there is any cost.

FIRST STEPS, MR./MRS. POLITICIAN

- $118,000,000 for programs to reduce opioid abuse
- $65,000,000 for a program to improve police-community relations
- $10,000,000 for the Byrne Criminal Justice Innovation Program
- $25,000,000 for justice reinvestment
- $22,500,000 for a body-worn camera partnership initiative; $500,000 for research and statistics on community trust (www.policegrantshelp.com)

What part of the money designated above will improve police-community relations? Justice reinvestment? Body-worn cameras, research, and Statistics?

When do we actually get some action-inspired grant money that is fueled by results-driven police work? Community feedback to ensure adequate exposure and distribution of the workload? So we know the money is there. We just have to actually use it for the listed intent and purpose instead of pushing another cause under the guise of police-community relations. Body-worn cameras, really?

The Office of Community-Oriented Policing Services

ARIZONA-2	ARKANSAS-1	CALIFORNIA-13	DELAWARE-1	FLORIDA-3
GEORGIA-1	ILLINOIS-1	INDIANA-1	MASSACHUSETTS-1	MICHIGAN-1
MINNESOTA-2	MISSOURI-2	NEW JERSEY-2	NEW YORK-1	NORTH CAROLINA-1
OHIO-3	OREGON-1	TEXAS-1	TRIBAL/ TERRITORIAL-1	UTAH-1
VIRGINIA-2	WISCONSIN-1			

So there are forty-three success stories to show for the grant money that has been given out so far? And I am afraid to see what time frame this covers.

Where do we get the audits of the agencies that are taking millions in grant money every year and don't have success stories to show for the money? If you make the money available to agencies who can show a success story and require a success story, then you will see real change.

The problem is that you have agencies such as the one I used to work for that will tell you without a doubt that community policing does not and will not work. That coming from a young sergeant right out of college who told me that he did a research paper in college and it would take far too much money to mandate community policing on a neighborhood and the end result could not be guaranteed.

He didn't want to hear about my experience with the housing authority and one other officer where we got a 74 percent drop in crime with minimal arrest and summons through a cooperation with the public and how you cannot mandate a policing program onto a neighborhood.

Monies are routinely given to strong arm policing because they require the use of new tactics that drive the law enforcement economies. Just look at the Atlanta Police Department website. In doing research for this book, I was looking up information and the first thing I saw on their website was a military-style helicopter with an officer getting ready to repel, I am assuming. Is that portraying a community friendly police department or one that is at war?

What message are we sending? Do we want your cooperation, or are we going to take it begrudgingly?

So what message are we sending?

VIRGINIA BILL TO KEEP OFFICERS' NAMES SECRET WOULD BE FIRST IN THE NATION, EXPERTS SAY

By Gary A. Harki and Patrick Wilson
The Virginian-Pilot

• Feb 18, 2016—A bill that would allow all Virginia law enforcement officers' names to be Mhthheld from the public would be the first of its kind in the country, police accountability and open records advocates say.

The proposal by Sen. John Cosgrove, R-Chesapeake—SB552—excludes the names of law enforcement and fire marshals from mandatory disclosure under the Virginia Freedom of Information Act and makes them a personnel record.

Cosgrove said he worked on the bill with the Fraternal Order of Police and the Virginia Association of Chiefs of Police. He acknowledged that officers' names could be secret "under the broadest scope of that bill."

It passed the Senate 25-15 this week and will soon be taken up by a House of Delegates subcommittee.

The bill is part of a growing movement inside the law enforcement community to shield officers from scrutiny after a rash of controversial police shootings around the country prompted protests and increased focus on officers, said Samuel Walker, professor emeritus of the School of Criminology and Criminal Justice at the

University of Nebraska Omaha and a longtime law enforcement scholar.

"This is part of the broader culture of shielding officers from being held accountable for their actions," Walker said. "And this is in the absence of any specific credible evidence that officers are targeted for that request. There's no basis for that position."

A bill before New Jersey lawmakers would allow officials to withhold the names of state police detectives. West Virginia lawmakers are considering a measure that shields officers' and their families' contact information from the public. And several states have or are examining laws aimed at preventing the release of the names of officers involved in shootings.

Norfolk Sheriff Bob McCabe said he thinks some officers' names—such as those working undercover—should be shielded from FOIA, but he does not agree with a broad exemption that hides all police names.

He, too, said the bill was a reaction to events such as the fatal shooting of unarmed teenager Michael Brown in Ferguson, Mo., in 2014. After that, the involved officer's life was threatened, McCabe said.

Police are more concerned than ever that someone will single them out to do them or their families harm, he said.

"I understand the intent of the bill, but I also understand the need for transparency," he said. "I haven't read the whole thing, but if it says that no names ever be accessible, that is a bit broad."

Cosgrove has given two rationales since submitting his bill Jan. 13.

"The reason I brought this forward: There was a court ruling in Norfolk. The Virginian-Pilot had requested this type of information—salary and position—and the court ruled that that was actually open to access," Cosgrove said in a Feb. 2 subcommittee hearing.

He said he was concerned about the safety of undercover officers and said "a brand-new rookie officer may one day be one of those detectives or undercover officers."

"I think this FOIA exemption is probably needed just because we want to make sure their safety is assured (and) their families are not put at risk just because their information as law enforcement officers is available."

The Virginian-Pilot requested the names and employment history of all law enforcement officers in the state from the Department of Criminal Justice Services to track officer movement from department to department. The newspaper is examining how often officers who got in trouble were able to find other jobs in law enforcement.

Megan Rhyne, executive director of the Virginia Coalition for Open Government, questioned how Cosgrove's theory would apply because undercover officers never use their real names while working in that capacity.

Later, Cosgrove began citing officer safety generally, saying public disclosure of the names of any officers could endanger them.

"My point is—and I used the San Antonio tabloid as the reason for doing this—if all of a sudden anybody goes and takes that information under FOIA, basically they can then publish it any way they want to. In San Antonio, they were going to publish the names and home addresses of all the San Antonio police force. I made the point very clear, that puts not only the law enforcement officer but most importantly their family in jeopardy."

The editor in chief of the San Antonio Observer, a free weekly, said Feb. 7 that the paper would look into publishing the names and addresses of all city police officers following an officer-involved shooting. The paper has since backed off the idea.

Cosgrove said he knew of no examples when asked for a time someone used public information to track down or commit violence against an officer.

"I don't have a particular instance of that," he said. "I'm sure that ones can be found. All you have to do is talk to any police department. They probably have a good illustration of that happening."

None of about a dozen people—law enforcement officers, legislators, academics, open government advocates—interviewed for this story could point to a case in which a police officer had been harmed because his name was found on a payroll sheet or other list of names.

Democratic Sen. John Miller of Newport News, a former journalist whose son was a state trooper and is now at the FBI, voted against Cosgrove's bill.

"I thought the bill was way too broad. The categories of people he wanted to exempt, like fire marshals, didn't need to be included," he said. "The public's paying their salaries, and they have a right to know that they're employed."

Other legislators thought Cosgrove made a compelling case.

"Having these records wide open, I think they're especially vulnerable, you know, for reactions from the public and that type of thing. They're out there doing a job, and I think it's altogether appropriate that we afford them that type of protection," said Sen. Frank Wagner, R-Virginia Beach. "They're out there, and they have a lot of enemies out there on the streets."

The full scope of Cosgrove's bill is unclear, such as whether officers' names could be redacted from crime reports.

Wayne Huggins, executive director of the Virginia State Police Association, a police union that lobbies the General Assembly, said he supports having police officers' identities completely secret.

"What we're trying to do is to move the ball to the greatest extent possible so as to provide protection and security for our folks," said Huggins, a former state police superintendent.

State police spokeswoman Corinne Geller declined to comment when asked why her agency publicizes names of troopers on its website. She said the Virginia State Police does not talk publicly about pending legislation.

If police names become secret, there is no way for the public to hold officers accountable, said Craig Futterman, a law professor at the University of Chicago who specializes in lights lawsuits and focuses on police brutality and racial discrimination.

"It is contrary to any notion of democracy or open governance," he said. "There are plenty of exemptions in eve1Y state to freedom of information acts that protect the safety and security of public employees. This is overly broad, sweeping and utterly unnecessary."

He called it contrary to a fundamental principal of policing: that the police are the public and the public are the police.

"Just in terms of community-police relationships and trust, how do police build relationships in their community if their names are secret?" he asked. "Police are special in a lot of ways. No other members of our government do we give the power to take away our freedom, the power to use force, the power to shoot and kill. Too much is at stake to let the police operate in secrecy."

Virginia's FOIA already has about 175 exemptions, and nearly all police reports are exempt from mandatory disclosure. The Center for Public Integrity, in a state report card, gives Virginia an "F" and ranks it 38th on access to public information.

Sen. Scott Surovell, a Democratic lawyer from Fairfax County, voted against Cosgrove's bill. His impression was that the national trend was "exactly the opposite."

"We want to see more transparency in law enforcement operations, not less. That's why you're seeing more and more jurisdictions in Virginia and outside Virginia adopting body cameras and dashboard cameras," he said.

"It's frightening to me that Virginia would be the first state in the United States to take this step."

The Associated Press contributed to this report.
Patrick Wilson, g04-697-1564, patrick.wilson@pilotonline.com
Gary A. Harki. 757-446-2370, guy.harki@pilotonkine.com
Will the Growing Militarization of Our Police Doom Community Policing? cops.usdoj.gov

Community policing, the author argues, does not necessarily empower the community but often increases the power of the police (www.press.umich.edu).

The conceptual ambiguity of community in community policing
Filtering the muddy waters
Mark E. Correia, Department of Criminal Justice,
University of Nevada, Reno, Nevada, USA

An important feature of community policing is the purposeful redefinition of certain democratic principles (Eck and Rosenbaum, 1994).

In terms of "effectiveness," emphasis no longer is placed on crime control through reactive methods (e.g. the ability of the police to solve and clear crimes); instead, effectiveness concerns the identification and solution of community problems. "Equity," which was previously defined as the equal treatment of citizens under the rule-of-law, now rests in the sharing of power with and the increased participation of community members.

While traditional policing agencies base "accountability" solely on the rule-of-law, community policing agencies are inclined to emphasize accountability in the context of the community they serve.

Last, for agencies practicing community policing, "efficiency" is defined as the police organization's ability to utilize community (i.e., governmental and non-governmental) resources to assist in problem-solving activities.

This contrasts sharply with the traditional law enforcement agency's notion of efficiency: the achievement of rapid response times to citizen complaints and calls for service at minimal taxpayer expense.

Essentially, this framework weaves community policing and community qualifies into a strong partnership allowing for the possible renewing fa sense of community and social capital, as well as strengthening the damaged social fabric and the establishment of "community" in America, thus helping to provide clarity in the conceptual muddy waters of community policing.

This is a portion of an article published in 2000.

CASE STUDIES

CASE 1—Officer Jason Vandyke Charged with Murder (Chicago PD)

Attorney Daniel Herbert, who confirmed he is representing Van Dyke, called the 14-year veteran a "highly decorated and well-regarded officer with zero discipline on his record."

"He believes he acted appropriately and within department guidelines," Herbert said.

Department records reviewed by the Tribune show that over the years, Van Dyke, who has been assigned mostly to high-crime neighborhoods, has been accused by citizens of a number of abuses, from hurling racial epithets to manhandling suspects and, in one complaint, pointing his gun at an arrestee without justification.

But he was never disciplined for any of the 15 complaints that have been resolved, including the one Nance filed after his run-in with Van Dyke, according to city documents obtained through a Freedom of Information Act request (Jason Meisner and Jeremy Gorner, *Chicago Tribune*, April 25, 2015).

Case 2—Officer Joshua Price—Charged with Stalking (Wichita, KS PD)

Jail records indicate that Joshua Price was arrested on suspicion of official misconduct; vehicle use by employee for personal gain and stalking intimate conduct cause fear to person/family. He is also listed on the Wichita police website as Officer Joshua R. Price. His arrest was by made by the Sedgwick County Sheriff (https://www.facebook.com/Wichitachief/posts/1598556220207972).

The woman said she reported the behavior to Price's lieutenant but she wasn't happy with the answer she received. She said she went to a substation the next morning and someone there directed her to the Professional Standards office within WPD. She would end up there several times in coming weeks.

"I went to professional standards, dealt with a couple of detectives and waited for them to do something. And nothing ever got done," she said.

She said Price was told not to contact her or her new boyfriend, but that didn't stop him. She said he or one of his partners was always around the home, circling the neighborhood or sitting across the street.

When the woman and Price were dating, she said the transmission on her vehicle went out. She said he was on a call one day and somehow became aware of a Jeep that was for sale. She said he sent her a picture of it and they picked it up the next weekend. She said he bought it for her.

Thursday, Oct. 19, the woman said she noticed someone broke into their new home and stole only her keys and Jeep.

"My Jeep was missing, and so was my keys and nothing else."

She didn't have proof it was Price but had her suspicions.

"I addressed what I had been going through," she said. "And as soon as the officer knew that there were cases with an officer, the captain came."

Her Jeep is still missing.

Case 3—Officer A. I. Geraldo—Relieved of Duty/Suspended (Miami-Dade PD)

In the video, a woman can be heard arguing with officers, one of whom tells her that she needs to be "corrected."

"Why do I have to be corrected when my life was just threatened and my daughter's (inaudible)?" the woman, later identified by police as Dyma Loving, says.

After Loving repeatedly tells the officers not to touch her, she is pulled to the ground by several officers. One of the officers appeared to put her in a headlock to get her to the ground.

"I wanted to call my kids," Loving tells officers. "My phone is dead."

The woman recording the video can be heard asking officers, "Why are you doing that?"

As the woman recording the video asks one of the officers for his name, he tells her, "Ma'am, I'm sorry. We're busy right now."

Loving, 26, was arrested on misdemeanor charges of disorderly conduct and resisting an office without violence.

Police said Loving and another woman, Adrianna Green, were walking past Tumm's home on Southwest 201st Street when Tumm, 50, called Green a "whore." Green told police she grabbed a plant from Tumm's yard and threw it at him, at which time Tumm grabbed a shotgun, pointed it at both women and threatened to shoot them.

The report identifies the officer who took Loving to the ground as A. I. Giraldo.

Perez said an immediate inquiry was initiated upon being made aware of the video. He said the officer was relieved of duty and of his role as a field training officer (by Peter Burke, Local10.com managing editor and Ian Margol, reporter).

Case 4—Names withheld—Case being investigated—(Philadelphia, Pa)

Philadelphia police are investigating after an officer was captured on video pulling a handcuffed woman by the hair and taking her down to the ground in North Philadelphia.

In the video, the officer stands behind eighteen-year-old Na-sha Lockett and presses her against a police cruiser as she repeatedly shouts at him, "Get the f——k off me!"

At one point, the officer says, "No," before Lockett shouts, "I'm about to spit on you!"

That's when the officer grabs her hair, pulls her head down and sweeps her leg to take her to the ground. As the officer tries to subdue her, she yells, "Get off me!"

The Philadelphia Police Department would not release the reason for the original stop, saying it is part of their Internal Affairs investigation.

"[The officers] were being disrespectful the whole time," Lockett said. "They could have done a little more. They could have asked questions."

Lockett said she spent the night in jail before disorderly conduct charges were dropped the next morning. The PPD, however, did not say whether or not charges may be pending (Rudy Chinchilla and Randy Gyllenhaal, published February 7, 2019, at 3:50 p.m., updated at 7:31 a.m. EST on February 8, 2019).

ABOUT THE AUTHOR

 KEVIN JOHNSON is a 21-1/2-year veteran of the police department, graduating from the Academy in 1995. In addition to primarily being a Community Police Officer, he participated in special assignments. "Project Cop" had him living in public housing to better understand the relationship between the neighborhood and the police. Another assignment was "Weed and Seed", a government-funded partnership between the public, Code Enforcement, Police, and the Court, the purpose of which was to identify and remove the "weeds" in particular neighborhoods and "seed" the good in the same. In its first year, Kevin, and a team of officers, was recognized as the Crisis Intervention Team equivalent to a team member. His passion for this field led him to become a Core Instructor for the CIT, where his focus was identifying the difference between a crime and a mental health situation. He was also a General Instructor and a Field Training Officer at the Police Academy.

Prior to becoming a police officer, Kevin was in the U.S. Army. He served in Desert Shield and subsequently Desert Storm as an Orthopaedical Technician in the 85th Evacuation Hospital in Dharan, Saudi Arabia, for which he received the Army Commendation Award. After his discharge from the Army, he joined the National Guard and, as a Corporal, served as a Field Medic from 1996-2002.

Kevin lives in Virginia with his wife Denise, he has 6 children, 6 grandchildren, 2 German Shepherds, and 2 Chihuahas.

CPSIA information can be obtained
at www.ICGtesting.com
Printed in the USA
BVHW040531210721
612410BV00015B/949